10-M

Home
Improvement

10-Minute
Home
Improvement

Hundreds of Fast Ways to Increase the Value of Your Home

Skye Alexander

FAIR WINDS
PRESS
GLOUCESTER, MASSACHUSETTS

Text © 2006 by Skye Alexander

First published in the USA in 2006 by
Fair Winds Press, a member of
Quayside Publishing Group
33 Commercial Street
Gloucester, MA 01930

10 09 08 07 06   1 2 3 4 5

ISBN - 13: 978-1-59223-218-2
ISBN - 10: 1-59233-218-8

Library of Congress Cataloging-in-Publication Data available

Original cover design by Laura Shaw
Cover illustration by Elizabeth Cornaro
Book design by Leslie Haimes

Printed and bound in USA

To Bill, who enjoys renovating old houses as much as I do.

TABLE OF CONTENTS

ACKNOWLEDGMENTS

Many thanks to all who offered ideas for this book, including Ron Conroy, Jimmy Holton, Myke and Al Perkins, Lyndsey Powers, E. Joe Deering, Anne Schneider, Elly Phillips, and especially my editor, Aimee Chase.

INTRODUCTION

I've always loved houses. And because my family moved every
year or so when I was growing up, I got to experience a lot of
different abodes, in many parts of the country. As a girl, I'd
knock on the door of any house I thought looked interesting
and ask the residents if they'd give me a tour, under the
pretenses of writing a term paper for school about local
architecture. Once I even got picked up for "breaking and
entering" when I couldn't resist crawling through an open
window of an abandoned antebellum mansion to look around.

(The police let me go, however, when they saw I hadn't damaged or stolen anything.)

My affection for architecture led me to study interior design in college. For many years after graduation, I worked as a residential and commercial interior designer, renovated homes of various styles and sizes, designed furniture, taught interior design at a Boston-area college, and wrote home-and-garden articles for numerous magazines and newspapers. Visiting "open houses" in nearby towns became my regular Sunday afternoon outing. When I went on vacation, I toured historic and celebrated homes—Newport's "cottages" and New Orleans' *maisons*, the fabulous Biltmore Estate and the starkly beautiful Shaker villages, Hawthorne's the House of the Seven Gables, and Elvis's Graceland.

In 1980, I bought a rundown antique house so I could learn firsthand how to do it myself. *This Old House* became my favorite TV show. More than a quarter-century later, I'm still remodeling old homes, and I can't walk into a building without mentally taking it apart and putting it back together again. This book offers ideas and information gleaned from my own experiences as well as tips from builders, architects, handymen, realtors, designers, and homeowners across the country. Because today's busy lifestyle doesn't always leave a lot of time for home improvement, I've included only upgrades that can be commissioned, researched, or accomplished in just ten minutes!

Seeing Your Home as Others See It

It's hard to be objective about our homes. Our homes not only provide shelter and a place to store our stuff, they serve as loci for family life, welcoming centers where we entertain friends, retreats when we need rest or privacy, repositories of memories, and links to our communities. For most of us, our homes are also our most valuable assets.

Quite literally, our homes are reflections of ourselves and reveal a great deal about us—as I quickly realized when I began practicing feng shui (the ancient Chinese art of placement) in

1987. Enter any residence, and you'll immediately get a sense of the people who live there—not only their tastes in home furnishings, but their lifestyles, interests, activities, habits, values, priorities, ages, income brackets, and so on.

Buying, furnishing, and rehabbing our homes, therefore, are very personal and emotional matters. No two individuals will do it in quite the same way. But while there may be no absolute right or wrong ways to proceed with home improvements, some approaches are more effective than others and are likely to result in greater comfort, convenience, charm, and/or market value. But while we may believe that, as homeowners or residents, we are best qualified to make decisions about how to update our living spaces, most of us can benefit from some professional advice, for several reasons.

- We don't undertake projects of this sort every day and might not be up to date on available products, techniques, and trends.
- Professional designers, architects, and building contractors understand the ins and outs of the business and can

facilitate a project, solve problems, and acquire items/
services we couldn't get on our own.

- We may have become so accustomed to living in a
particular way that we don't realize there might be better
possibilities.
- We may not be able to honestly and dispassionately
evaluate our homes—our emotional attachments can cloud
our perspective.
- If you plan to sell your home in the near future, or are
updating investment property for resale or rental, it's
important to learn which updates will fetch the greatest
return.

Surviving Home Improvements

Although change can be exciting and the final results are usually worth the effort, the process itself is often stressful. Eating out every day while your kitchen is being remodeled may sound like fun, but it gets old fast—especially with young children. Having workmen, noise, mess, and disorder in your private sanctuary day after day can test the sanity of even the most patient person.

Whether you do the work yourself or hire other people to handle it for you, be prepared to experience impatience, frustration, irritability, and emotional upsets while your living space undergoes a transformation. Be gentle with yourself and your housemates during this chaotic period. Minimize stress in other areas of your life while you're rehabbing your home; pick a time when your workload is light or when the kids are away at summer camp. Design an "escape strategy," whether it's living elsewhere while the messiest work is going on, taking weekend vacations to get away from it all, or treating yourself to regular trips to the spa.

Planning ahead, of course, is the most important part of updating your home. This book has two objectives: to help reduce the confusion and complications that accompany home improvements and to offer aesthetic as well as practical suggestions that can make your home more comfortable, attractive, and valuable.

PART ONE

The Basics

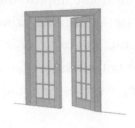

CHAPTER 1

Floor Plans and *Your* Plans

It's been said that the only constant is change. That's certainly true when it comes to our homes. As soon as we move into a new residence—sometimes even before—we begin making changes. We paint walls, tear up old linoleum, replace light fixtures, and plant shrubs. The popularity of TV shows, such as PBS's *This Old House* and those aired on HGTV (Home and Garden Television) and the DIY (Do-It-Yourself) Network, attests to our passion for home improvements. In recent years, the number of home-and-garden magazines has burgeoned—Amazon.com offers subscriptions to more than 350, with *Martha Stewart Living* in the number one spot. Home store chains that sell building supplies continue to proliferate and show healthy profits.

If you're like most Americans, you'll probably make some changes in your living space this year. Maybe you've purchased an older house that needs some updates, or your kids have left the nest and you want to convert a bedroom into an office. Perhaps your home suffered damage in a storm, or it's just looking a little tired and needs some refurbishing. Or maybe you're planning to sell and figure that a bit of sprucing up will help you fetch a better price for your property. Regardless of the improvements you intend to make, **proper planning and clarifying your objectives ahead of time will enable you to save money, time, and aggravation.**

Know Thyself

Updating your home may seem to be a practical, rational, logical endeavor, but start ripping out kitchen cabinets, hanging wallpaper, or shopping for paint colors and you'll soon notice how emotional the process is. Turning a grown child's bedroom into a home office may trigger empty-nest sadness or fears about aging. Repairing damage done by a fire could stir up feelings related to the trauma. Power struggles can erupt between household members over whether to purchase a new sound system or sofa.

Many of our choices are emotionally based, too. You might decide to install a wood-burning stove or claw-foot bathtub because they remind you of Grandma's country cottage. An intelligent, educated woman I know opted for lots of built-in bookcases in her living room, even though it was more convenient to store her books in her office, because books symbolize the self-image she wants to convey to all who visit her home.

It's important to clarify your objectives before you begin knocking down walls and buying appliances. Ask yourself some basic questions:

- Are you making updates for your own benefit or to maximize your home's resale value?
- Are you making changes for practical reasons or aesthetic ones?
- What's your time frame for starting and completing the work?
- How much money have you budgeted for updates?
- What do you hope to gain as a result of the changes you make?
- What do you consider essential and what's optional?
- Are your objectives short-term or long-term?
- Will you be making improvements in stages, over a period of time, or all at once?
- How much can you do yourself and what will require professional help?
- What outcome do you envision?

• What plans do you have for adjusting your lifestyle while work is taking place in your home?

When a partner, roommate, or family member is involved in the process, decision-making can become more complicated. Many couples have very different ideas, needs, preferences, and tastes. If the proposed changes will affect one person more greatly than another, perhaps that person's concerns and choices should bear more weight. For instance, if one member of a family does most of the cooking, his/her decisions about how to redo the kitchen are paramount.

Determine your priorities. It might help to make individual lists and rank the items each of you considers important; you may be surprised to discover what matters most to whom, and why. If you have your heart set on hardwood floors in the living room and your partner really wants granite countertops, incorporate these features into your plans, so that everyone gets at least some of the things they desire.

Be willing to compromise. When you can't agree, try to find an alternative that's acceptable to all concerned. If your partner wants to paint the master bedroom pink and you insist that blue is a better choice, maybe you can settle on yellow.

As in every area of life, your attitude about making home improvements will greatly influence the experience. **View renovation as an adventure. Accept that you will encounter surprises and challenges along the way.** Take advantage of the learning opportunities that arise. Be flexible. Pay attention to details, but don't get caught up in them; keep your eye on the goal. Undergoing home improvements is like giving birth—once the mission is accomplished, you usually forget about the discomfort inherent in the process.

Homework: Repair, Remodel, Restore, Renovate

Based on the kind of home you live in, the amount of care your home needs, the budget you're working with, and your overall objective, you'll want to consider all four of these methods of home improvement.

Repairs are a fact of home ownership. Older houses tend to need more upkeep than new ones, and antique buildings are like spoiled children—they never stop demanding attention. Although some repairs can be delayed, they can't be avoided and ignoring them may lead to other problems and costs. Most home repairs should be handled in the same way as a decayed tooth; the sooner you do something the better.

Remodeling is generally optional. That burnt orange countertop in the kitchen and that black and pink tile in the bathroom may be perfectly functional, but they're dated. We're a consumer culture that delights in the new. We grow tired of looking at the same surroundings year after year, the same way we get bored wearing the same clothes. Like elective surgery, most remodeling projects can be approached at your own pace, so take time to determine what you want to do and why. Gather data, shop around, do research, interview contractors, and get prices. Peruse magazines and go to open houses to get ideas. Contact manufacturers and ask them to send you literature. Collect pictures, resources, fabric and paint samples, and other information.

Restoration means bringing an older building back to its original (or close to original) state. Period details—wainscoting, moldings, wooden ceiling beams, hardware, etc.—that once existed should be replaced as faithfully as possible, sometimes using parts from similar houses of the same era and/or style.

Renovation frequently involves both necessary repairs and cosmetic remodeling. It can range from extensive refurbishing to a complete overhaul. Renovation may be done to restore an older home with architectural merit, to repair significant damage due to fire, neglect, or an "act of God," or to convert a structure from one type of use to another (from a large single-family to condos, for instance). Although renovating a home can be extremely rewarding, it's time-consuming, expensive, and disruptive. Unless you are adventurous, persevering, patient, and adaptable, and you possess some construction skills, I don't recommend doing it yourself.

In 1980, my former husband and I began renovating our first house, a twelve-room, three-story Greek Revival in one of

Salem, Massachusetts's historic districts. Built in 1847, this handsome antique had served as subsidized housing for low-income families for many years and had deteriorated to a pathetic state. By the time we finished renovating it—doing all of the work ourselves—the only original features that remained were the fireplaces, wood floors, and slate roof, and even those had been improved upon. At various times during the rehab, we lived without plumbing, heat, interior walls, and ceilings. Sometimes we camped out in a single room while the rest of the house was in chaos. In the process, we learned to lay tile, blow insulation, sweat pipes, sand floors, install kitchen cabinets, stud walls, tape wallboard, hang windows and doors, build decks, and replace rotten sills. More than twenty-five years later, we're both still renovating houses, for ourselves and other homeowners.

The Good, the Bad, and the Ugly

All buildings have assets and drawbacks; there's some Beauty and some Beast in every home. The goal is to highlight the positive aspects and downplay the negative. Start with the obvious. Does your location afford you a terrific view? Capitalize on it. Put in new, larger windows or French doors. Cut down a few trees or clear out brush. Does your house boast decorative exterior trim? Highlight it by painting the walls one color and the trim a contrasting color. Or strip off old paint and restore the wood's natural luster.

In one antique home I renovated, the master bedroom's fireplace had been covered over with wallboard. We removed the wallboard and exposed not only the hidden fireplace, but also the old brick chimney all the way up to the ceiling. Then we scoured antique shops until we found an attractive, eighteenth-century pine mantelpiece that fit, to transform an ordinary room into a cozy haven rich with character.

Most likely, your home has a few flaws, too. Older houses rarely afford enough closets—either add a few or revamp the ones you have by adjusting clothing rods and shelving to better utilize storage space. Outdated windows are a common complaint, too—replace them with energy-efficient ones. Open up cramped bedrooms under the house's eaves by adding dormers. You might be able to fit in a half-bath under the stairs or knock down a wall between two small bedrooms to create a gracious master suite.

Take a tour of your own home, as if you were seeing it for the first time, to evaluate its pluses and minuses. In a notebook, create a section for "assets" and another for "drawbacks." As you walk through each room, carefully note the good or potentially positive features your home offers in the "assets" section. Then, write down all the problems or things you just don't like in the "drawbacks" section. If you don't feel you can be objective, ask a friend or relative whose opinion you trust—or a real estate agent if you're planning to sell—to accompany you.

When you've completed your inventory, rank the drawbacks according to priority. Repairs that should be fixed immediately and little things you can take care of easily will go at the top of your list. Minor annoyances or major updates you can't afford to do right now might fall near the bottom. Next, examine your home's good points and potential plusses. Can some of the drawbacks be improved upon so they also accentuate the positives, such as adding a window to brighten a dark room *and* take advantage of a nice view? Can you remedy the "beast" *and* emphasize "beauty" simultaneously, such as tearing out a water-damaged ceiling and adding a dormer?

As you organize your list, you'll realize that some improvements can't be done until others are completed; for instance, you can't wallpaper the living room until the new windows have been installed. You'll also see how one repair may lead to another. Once you remove those old fluorescent overhead fixtures in the kitchen, for example, you'll have to patch and paint the ceiling. Analyzing your home in this manner helps you assess and organize your objectives. It also enables you to prepare a work list, budget, and timeline. Bringing your tasks into perspective this way can make them seem less daunting.

Common Remodeling Mistakes

Old House Journal runs a popular feature called "Remuddling" in each issue, which shows some amazingly awful updates that clumsy contractors and clueless homeowners have implemented. Although these atrocities are the worst of the worst, you can drive through any town's up-and-coming old neighborhoods and spot a spate of remodeling woes. Here are some common no-no's to avoid.

Exterior
- Removing original, decorative trim when applying new siding
- Putting vinyl siding on an antique building
- Installing windows that are the wrong size or type for the building's style or period
- Hanging shutters that are too small for the windows
- Putting on a front door that is out of character with the house

- Adding a garage that is so prominent it overshadows or detracts from the house
- Destroying the original roof line to add a dormer
- Putting up a fence that is out of character with the house
- Cutting down too many trees or removing too much of the natural vegetation
- Adding a porch that's too small or a deck that's too large for the house

Interior

- Putting a Cadillac kitchen in a Chevy house
- Installing inexpensive molded plastic tub and shower surrounds in bathrooms
- Laying vinyl flooring that imitates wood
- Hanging hollow-core interior doors
- Hanging doors that open the wrong way
- Putting skimpy or unimaginative stock woodwork in a higher-end house or condo

- Not providing easy access to plumbing
- Insulating only part of the building
- Making a building so airtight that there's inadequate air exchange
- Updating one bathroom but not the other(s)
- Painting everything off-white

Show and Sell

Are you planning to put your home on the market in the near future? In 2005, more than 7 million "housing units"—houses, townhouses, condominiums, and co-ops—were sold in the United States. New single-family houses accounted for approximately 1.3 million of these sales, up from about 877,000 in 2000. Although housing prices vary significantly from one part of the country to another, the national median price for a single-family house was $230,200 in 2005, up from $166,540 in 2000. Experts such as David Lereah, chief economist for the National Association of Realtors, believe housing sales and prices could decline in the coming years due to increases in the cost of fuel, especially in the Northeast and Midwest. But as Baby Boomers retire and snowbirds move to warmer regions, the housing industry in the South and Southwest is likely to experience new growth.

If you intend to sell your home within the year, making some updates could help you get a better price for your property and/or sell it faster. However, the improvements you undertake might be quite different if your goal is to sell your home rather than if you plan to stay put for a while. For example, you probably wouldn't paint the living room purple or put a $9,000 Aga range in a home you're going to sell soon. But replacing cracked windowpanes, installing new kitchen countertops, or refinishing wood floors could be smart choices.

Your location, the amount of time and money you have to invest, your home's price bracket, and numerous other factors will undoubtedly influence your decisions. Statistics indicate, though, that some repairs and renovations are more likely to pay dividends than others. Most sources agree that updating kitchens and bathrooms are the most profitable investments. According to popular TV show host Bob Vila, the biggest paybacks in older homes result from adding or upgrading features to meet standards in new homes, including central air conditioning, master bedroom suites, and energy efficient windows. Refinishing wood floors and adding closets tend to be good investments, too. *SmartMoney* magazine says that in higher-end homes—especially in the West and outhwest—outdoor fireplaces, indoor hot tubs, personal spas, granite countertops, and cathedral ceilings are trendy updates.

Here's a breakdown of what you can expect to recoup, on average, from the most popular home improvements.

IMPROVEMENT PAYBACK

Remodel a bathroom (no frills)	81 to 87 percent
Add a full bathroom (no frills)	89 to 120 percent
Remodel a master bed/bath suite	82 percent
Remodel a kitchen	79 to 85 percent
Add a fireplace	126 percent
Put on new siding	68 to 85 percent
Add a room	68 to 83 percent
Add insulation	68 to 79 percent
New roof	77 percent
Install skylights	77 percent
Replace windows and/or doors	68 to 69 percent
Add a wood deck	71 percent
Convert a room to a home office	58 percent
Add a swimming pool	31 to 40 percent

Of course, some updates will generate better returns in some parts of the country, and in some neighborhoods, than others. Swimming pools aren't likely to be as big a draw in Maine as in Florida. A new heating system will score more points in Wisconsin than in Arizona. In crowded Northeastern cities, off-street parking is precious. Southwesterners prize their RV barns. Overall, however, reasonable home improvements only return on average about seventy-five cents on the dollar. Therefore, **the main reason for remodeling your home should be to please yourself and to improve the quality of your domestic life.**

Must-Dos

Some home improvements and repairs may not garner any profits at all. Home buyers expect certain features—a sound roof, an up-to-date plumbing system, a garage door that operates smoothly. Although some updates are optional, many repairs must be taken care of before you sell your home. Most home buyers opt to have a professional inspect a property before purchasing it, and they will use any problems that turn up to try to reduce the asking price of your home. Particularly if housing sales are sluggish in your area and/or the market is saturated with inventory, it's in your best interest to fix the following problems before you begin showing your home:

- Inadequate or failed septic system
- Outdated or poorly operating heating and air conditioning system
- Wet basement
- Leaky roof
- Insect infestation
- Visible dry rot
- Rusted or outdated electrical box
- Water marks on ceilings or walls
- Leaky toilets and/or faucets
- Stained bathtub
- Broken tile around tub and shower
- Cracked windowpanes
- Windows with broken seals

- Damaged locks
- Broken steps or railings on a porch/deck

Optional Updates

While not mandatory, the following improvements could add visual appeal to your home and increase its resale value:

- Repair a nonworking fireplace
- Add a decorative propane or electric fireplace-stove
- Replace an old, outdated bathroom vanity and sink
- Replace old linoleum on the kitchen floor with ceramic tile
- Give your home a fresh coat of paint—inside and out
- Put in some attractive shrubs/flowers/landscaping

Fast Fixes

These easy, inexpensive fix-ups give prospective buyers a positive first impression of your home. Minor problems can arouse suspicion, making buyers think that a home hasn't been well maintained and causing them to look more closely for other flaws. Take care of the following before you put your property on the market:

- Clean up debris in the yard
- Trim hedges and shrubs
- Adjust doors that stick, especially the front door
- Wash windows
- Replace burned-out light bulbs
- Re-glue peeling wallpaper
- Shampoo carpeting
- Buff wood floors
- Re-grout around tub and shower
- Fasten dangling electrical wires into place
- Replace torn screens
- Fix loose shingles on the roof
- Repair a broken or sagging fence
- Replace inoperable locks

More to Come

Throughout Part Two, I've included special boxed tips and ideas labeled "Show & Sell" that are specifically intended for those of you who'll soon be selling your homes. Some of these suggestions come from real estate agents, builders, designers, and architects across the country—people who have their fingers on the pulse of the home-buying public. You'll also find boxed tips called "Fast Fixes," little things that count big but don't take much time at all, and "Product Picks," special products that allow you to make the most of each home improvement.

CHAPTER 2

Inside Information

You are about to embark on an exciting adventure, one that may involve quite a bit of time, energy, and money. These resources are precious, so you don't want to waste them. Nor do you want to make unnecessary mistakes that could delay your project or blow your budget. You can't foresee every challenge that will arise during your home improvement odyssey, but good planning and preparation can help you avoid a lot of headaches along the way.

Before You Begin

Most communities have enacted certain rules, regulations, and requirements for home building and remodeling. To prevent problems, it's a good idea to familiarize yourself with the laws that pertain to your particular project—before you begin work.

Building Codes

Building codes are regulations established by local authorities to govern various aspects of residential and commercial building. Codes differ from region to region, state to state, and even town to town, and they change periodically. Although most building codes are enacted for public safety reasons, some seem to have been put into place rather arbitrarily. Sometimes codes apply to one type of home, but not another. Condos and multifamily buildings often have different requirements than single-family houses. In some cases, antique or historic structures may be allowed to waive certain code requirements that aren't feasible or would destroy their architectural significance.

Some features that usually must comply with specific building codes are electricity and wiring, plumbing, septic and waste removal systems, fireplaces and wood stoves, heating and air conditioning systems, natural gas appliances and hook-ups, water treatment systems, and foundations and structural elements. For instance, ground fault circuit interrupting electrical outlets or "GFCIs" need to be installed near sinks to prevent the possibility of electrocution. Wood-burning stoves must be placed a safe distance from combustible surfaces to reduce the risk of fire. The Boston area is one where smoke alarms are required in residences and commercial buildings. New smoke detectors have to be electrically hard-wired together so they all go off in sequence and must be installed at specific locations on each floor of your home. Before you can sell a house or condo, the local fire inspector must test your "smokes" and issue a certificate saying that they are up to code.

Before you undertake significant improvements in your home, check with your local building inspector to determine what codes exist in your area. Depending on the type of work you're doing, you may also need to get guidelines or permission from your community's department of public works, fire department, historic commission, zoning board, or other regulatory agency.

Be sure to check your plot plan and/or deed, too, if the improvements you intend to make will expand the footprint of your home. You don't want to infringe on an abutter's property. It's also a good idea to discuss your plans with your neighbors, if the project will have a visual or auditory impact on them. A few years ago, one of my neighbors built a swimming pool, which required extensive blasting, tree cutting, grading, and months of noisy construction. His insensitivity regarding the annoyance his project caused led to a great deal of animosity in the neighborhood.

Permits

Usually, it's necessary to acquire a building permit before you begin doing work on your home. If a building contractor, architect, electrician, plumber, carpenter, or other professional is handling your updates, he or she will take care of this detail. If you're doing it yourself, you'll need to get the required permits yourself. If you don't acquire a permit and get caught doing work that falls under your community's regulations, you could be fined.

Contact the department of public works or city hall in your community to find out where you must apply for a permit. You'll probably be asked to submit a written description of the work you intend to do on your property. You might have to include drawings, photos, diagrams, or other detailed information as well. The fee for the permit is usually based on the estimated cost of the improvements you're making. For example, a friend of mine who recently installed a $20,000 forced hot water heating system in his house in Ipswich, Massachusetts, paid $75 for the relevant permit. Display the permit in a window or other easily visible spot while the updates are taking place.

A building inspector may visit the site before issuing a permit in order to assess the project, especially if you plan to do extensive renovations or if your improvements could affect your neighbors. At various stages of the project, the inspector may return to check your progress. When the job is complete, the inspector will come back and okay your work.

Some repairs and updates don't require a permit. For instance, you don't usually have to pull a permit to paint your house or hang new shutters. However, if you live in an historic district, you may need to submit paint samples and a detailed description to the local historic commission for approval. In some instances, you may be able to make repairs to an existing structure, but can't tear down the old building and erect a new one without a permit. It's always wise to check the rules and regulations in your area prior to beginning work, just to be on the safe side.

Applying for a building permit alerts your city or county appraisal office to the fact that your home is undergoing improvements. Usually an appraiser will visit your home after the work has been completed and will reassess your home's value based on the updates you've made. In most instances, you can expect your property taxes to increase accordingly.

Contractors

Many improvements, such as adding insulation, building a deck, or installing new windows, can be made by the home-owner. Your community may require electrical and plumbing projects, however, to be handled by a licensed professional. But how can you find a reliable, capable, honest contractor with whom you feel comfortable working?

We've all heard horror stories about building contractors; many of us have experienced nightmares ourselves. Common complaints include poor workmanship, cost overruns, lengthy delays, no-shows, damage to homeowners' property, even scam artists who pocketed sizable deposits and never did a lick of work. I've served as a juror in two cases against incompetent and crooked contractors, and had first-hand experience with more than a few.

The best way to find a good building contractor is to ask friends, relatives, neighbors, or coworkers for a referral. You may also contact the National Association of the Remodeling Industry, the Remodelors Council of the National Association of Home Builders, the American Society of Home Inspectors, or the American Institute of Architects for information. Your state's licensing board can tell you if a contractor is licensed and the Better Business Bureau will know if a contractor has received complaints from other customers.

HomeRemodelingOnline.com provides useful tips for choosing a contractor. ImproveNet.com, another online service, provides information about contractors' backgrounds. On AngiesList.com, homeowners rate plumbers, electricians, landscapers, handymen, etc. in thirty-one major U.S. cities.

Before you hire a contractor, ask to see examples of his or

her work. Even if the contractor gets rave reviews from former customers, he or she may not be right for you. Someone who specializes in contemporary tract homes, for instance, might not be sensitive to the peculiarities associated with antique cottages. Interview more than one potential contractor before you make a decision. Get detailed, written quotes from them; prices could vary significantly. Some contractors will allow homeowners to participate in the remodeling project and do part of the work themselves, which could save you money; others insist on handling the job completely themselves.

Many general contractors work with subcontractors who perform certain facets of a remodeling or renovation project. The GC oversees the entire operation, but may sub out the tile work, countertops, or heating system to an independent specialist. General contractors don't necessarily handle every step of a job, such as installing carpet. Find out what your contractor will and won't do. If there's someone you'd like to use for a particular task—maybe you know a great paperhanger or a cabinetmaker who crafts beautiful crown moldings—make sure your contractor doesn't have a problem working with him or her.

Discuss insurance issues with prospective contractors. Any contractors you hire should be insured in case someone accidentally spills paint on your antique Persian rug or improperly installs the washing machine and floods your basement. Make sure the general contractor also carries medical insurance to cover himself or herself and the people who work for him or her, as well as workman's compensation, so that you won't be held responsible if someone is hurt on the job. (Depending on where you live and other circumstances, you still could end up paying for injuries or could be sued if an accident occurs on your property. Check with your homeowners insurance agent to see if you need to purchase additional insurance while workers are in your home.) Find out, too, if your contractor and his or her employees and subs are bonded. This means the contractor carries a type of insurance to reimburse you in case he or she doesn't perform the work satisfactorily or is responsible for damage to your property. Your city hall should keep records of the bonded contractors in your area.

Working with Contractors

Once you've chosen a general contractor to oversee your project, draw up a contract and work out a schedule together. Get everything in writing! Be as clear, careful, and specific as possible. Create a punch list and check off pieces of the project as they are completed. The more organized you are in the beginning, the fewer snags you'll run into later on. If you don't understand something, ask for clarification. If your contractor isn't receptive to your input or balks at being pinned down, find another contractor. This is the "honeymoon stage" and if you aren't communicating effectively now, you could end up battling things out in court at some future date.

Agree on products and materials to be used. If you want a particular brand of windows or hardware, stipulate it. I always prepare a room-by-room spec sheet that lists every item to be included—manufacturer/brand, style, color/finish, size, etc. Solicit your contractor's opinions, but don't turn over the decision-making to him or her—unless you really don't care. Although a building contractor may be competent at the hands-on stuff, I've met very few who possess much aesthetic sensibility.

Determine a time frame in which the work will be performed and completed. The schedule you and your contractor decide on should outline the different stages of your home improvement project and how long each stage is likely to take. Some parts of the job can't begin until others are finished. Delays are one of the most frequent remodeling complaints. Some delays are unavoidable or aren't your contractor's fault. Weather conditions may prevent work from moving forward or interfere with shipping; materials may not be available or may not be delivered promptly, especially if they're coming from another country. However, it's common for builders and subs to work on more than one job site at a time. Your project could get upstaged by someone else's. Workers don't always show up when they're supposed to either.

When you sign a contract, you'll be required to put down a deposit, usually a quarter to a third of the total price of the job. Establish a schedule whereby you make additional payments as the work progresses. Hold back a certain amount until everything is finished as agreed upon; **never pay a contractor the full amount up front.** You may wish to include a clause in your agreement that financially penalizes the contractor if the project takes significantly longer than estimated. Or you could use the carrot approach and tack on a bonus if the job is completed ahead of time and to your satisfaction.

Of course, situations you can't foresee will arise. Once you start tearing into walls and floors, especially in older homes, you are likely to discover problems that weren't apparent at first. Sills may be rotten, or old wiring may need to be replaced. Some flexibility will be necessary on your part. **Murphy's Law usually applies to home improvements; expect the job to cost more and take longer than you initially thought it would.**

Trade Terminology

The key to knowing (and getting) exactly what you want from your contractor is to learn their professional lingo. Here is a list of commonly used home-improvement terms to help you communicate effectively:

Argon: gas used between windowpanes for insulating purposes

Backsplash: a vertical extension at the back of a countertop to protect the wall, usually four inches high

Beam: supporting structure in an attic or floor

Blueboard: a special type of wallboard used in bathrooms and wet areas

Bullnose: rounded edge for a counter or tabletop

COM: customer's own material; usually refers to fabric supplied by the customer for use on furniture, window treatments, walls, etc.

Elevation: a scale drawing showing a straight-on view of a wall

Fixture: in a bathroom the tub, sink, and toilet are referred to as fixtures; electric lights are also called fixtures

Floor plan: a scale drawing showing a bird's-eye view of your home's layout

Footprint: the space your house occupies on the land

French door: framed glass door that's hinged, often hung as a pair

GC: general contractor; person responsible for overseeing the project

GFCI: Ground fault circuit interruptor; a grounded electrical outlet, used near a sink or other wet areas to prevent the risk of electrocution

Grille: dividers between windowpanes

Hardware: doorknobs, handles, hinges, etc.

HVAC: Heating, ventilation, air conditioning; central heating/air conditioning system

Jamb: surrounding frame for a door

Joist: supporting structure in an attic or floor that ties into a beam

Light: window glass; sidelights run beside a door

Mud: mortar into which tile, brick, stone, etc. is set

Ogee: decorative S-shaped edge for a counter, tabletop, or other surface

Pier and beam: foundation technique using upright supports (piers) and cross pieces (beams) in a building that has no basement, raising the building off the ground to provide a crawl space beneath

Plot plan: scale diagram of your plot or property, showing buildings, driveway, right of ways, etc.

PVC: Polyvinylchloride; "plastic" pipe used in plumbing

Sash: frame around a windowpane

Siding: material used on the exterior of your home (clapboard, shingles, vinyl, masonry, etc.)

Sill: supporting timber at the base of an outer wall, on which the wall rests

Slab: concrete foundation for a house with no basement

Soffit: boxed portion of a wall that houses electricity, air vents, ductwork, etc.

Specs: specifications or details of the project

Subcontractor: subs; people often hired by the GC to perform certain specialized parts of a project, such as electrical work

Subflooring: material, such as plywood, used as a base underneath tile, vinyl flooring, or carpet

Stud: wood or metal upright structural support inside a wall, onto which wallboard (or other wall material) is attached

Transom: window positioned above a door

Wallboard (gypsum board, sheetrock): material generally used for interior walls

Sizing Up Your Space

You can save yourself a lot of wasted time, effort, and money by creating a plan on paper, before you begin. Whether you're completely rehabbing your home or just buying new furniture, first measure your space and sketch it to scale.

Drawing a Floor Plan

If you intend to handle all or part of the job yourself, one of your first tasks will be to draw a floor plan of your home. This may seem like a highly involved project, but if you break it into these smaller steps, you'll be able to fit it into your busy schedule.

Step one: Decide if you'd rather draw your floor plan by hand or use a computer program.

Step two: If you're using paper, gather the following materials:

- Tape measure (25-feet or longer)
- Graph paper (the sheets should be printed with quarter-inch squares)
- Tracing paper (optional)
- Pencil
- Ruler or architect's scale
- Transparent or masking tape (optional)
- Three-ring binder or expandable file

If you're using the computer, search the Internet for a useful guide to creating your own floor plan. The site www.homegarden.move.com for example, provides easy-to-follow instructions for creating both floor plans and elevations. (At the site, look for the section on "Tools and Articles for Buying, Moving, and Improving." Select "Improve

Your Home," then "Remodeling," then "Planning," then "Put It on Paper.") If you'd rather work on the computer, download software that allows you to create your own customized floor plan; www.smartdraw.com is one good option. Hint: In order to see both the current layout and the new and improved layout, you'll want to create a before floor plan and an after floor plan.

Step three: Choose a floor of your home or an area of your home to depict in the floor plan.

Step four: Perform the measurements required to create your floor plan.

Step five: Draw your before floor plan on the graph paper using either a scale of one-quarter inch equals one foot or one-half inch equals one foot, or craft it using computer software and print it out.

Step six: Do the same for your after floor plan, using tracing paper if you'd like to be able to place it on top of your before floor plan to compare them.

Step seven: Position the after drawing beside or, if you used tracing paper, on top of the before drawing so that you can clearly see how the proposed changes will alter the current configuration.

Step eight: Consider the traffic patterns that will be created by your changes. How will people move about in your home? Start at the entrance and draw lines on your diagram to indicate the paths you and household members will use as you navigate this area of your home. Ask yourself whether the proposed changes will afford you greater comfort and convenience. If not, make adjustments as necessary.

Step nine: Place your floor plans in a three-ring binder or expandable file. Store them in a safe place. As time goes on, you may want to add magazine pictures, manufacturers' literature, paint/wallpaper samples, and other ideas to the binder or file.

Step ten: Take it shopping! The floor plan you've created lets you see instantly whether that oversized soaking tub or three-piece sectional sofa you're considering will fit into your space.

Drawing Elevations

In addition to a floor plan, you may wish to make another set of drawings called elevations. These are scale diagrams that show a straight-on view of each interior and/or exterior wall. Elevations allow you to see the alignment of doors and windows, the heights of countertops and cabinets, the positioning of stairways, variations in floors or ceiling heights, and architectural features. You can use elevations to design any room— or any portion of a room such as a built-in bookcase, balcony, fireplace, or deck. Now that you're armed with all the materials you used to draw your floor plan, choose a room or a portion of a room that you'd like to improve upon and create an elevation using the following steps.

Step one: Measure the height and width of each wall that will be altered by your proposed updates, or simply follow the dimensions on your floor plan. Draw the rectangle (or other shape if the wall isn't a rectangle) on the graph paper, to scale. You can use either a scale of one-quarter inch equals one foot or, if you wish to include more detail, try a scale of one-half inch equals one foot.

Step two: Sketch in whatever features you plan to include in your updates—doors, windows, counters, stairs, fireplaces, etc.—to scale. Now you can see how the various elements relate to one another, whether they seem harmonious or incongruous.

Step three: You may wish to include pieces of furniture in your elevation drawings. This enables you to see whether your bureau will fit under the new window you plan to install or if the back of that Shaker settee will line up with the proposed wainscoting.

Step four: If you intend to make changes in both the interior and the exterior of your home, consider doing elevations to show how the updates will alter both the inside and the outside appearance. On the exterior renderings, include such things as shutters, siding, shrubs, etc. to give you as accurate a picture as possible of the end result.

Step five: You may wish to do larger, detailed sketches of special features such as trim moldings, countertop edges, tile work, railings, etc.

Step six: Add these sketches to your three-ring binder or expandable file.

Table of Standard Measurements

As you draw your plans, keep the following dimensions in mind. If you've decided to include (or are considering) certain items such as doors, windows, kitchen cabinets, and appliances, ask the manufacturer to provide you with exact specifications.

Walls: Interior walls are usually about $4^1/_2$ inches thick, exterior walls about $6^1/_2$ inches thick. The walls of older homes may vary, depending on construction techniques and materials. Siding (stone, brick, adobe, etc.) can alter the walls' thickness.

Ceilings: Usually ceilings are 96 inches (8 feet) high. Homes built before 1800 may have lower ceilings; those built during the mid-1800s to 1920s may have higher ceilings. Cathedral ceilings may be 12 feet high or more. In some warm climates, such as New Orleans, homes may feature high ceilings to dissipate the heat, whereas New England antiques were often constructed with low ceilings to retain heat.

Doors: Standard doors are 30 to 36 inches wide by 80 inches high, but closet doors and some interior doors may be narrower. Hinged patio/French doors are 24 to 36 inches wide, each door. Sliding patio door sets are 60 to 96 inches wide, both doors. Wheelchair access requires a minimum width of 32 inches, although 34 is even better.

Closets: At a minimum closets, must be 24 inches deep. For bedroom closets, allow a minimum of 30 inches deep by 48 inches wide, per person. Bathroom, linen, and broom closets should be at least 18 inches wide by 18 inches deep.

Kitchen cabinets: Base cabinets are usually 24 inches deep by 34 1/2 inches high. Upper or wall cabinets are 12 inches deep by 24, 30, or 36 inches high. Individual cabinet widths range from about 9 to 48 inches and are usually sized in 3-inch increments.

Countertops: Usually these are 25 inches deep by 1 1/2 inches thick. Kitchen countertops are positioned at a height of 36 inches, whether on base cabinets or other supports; bar countertops are usually 42 inches high; backsplashes attached to countertops are typically 4 inches high.

Bathtubs: Basic tubs are generally about 60 inches long by 30 inches wide by 15 inches high. Whirlpool or spa tubs range from the size of an ordinary bathtub up to 48 by 84 inches. Soaking tubs tend to be deeper, up to 72 inches long by 30 inches high.

Bathroom vanities: Most range from about 24 to 60 inches wide by 21 inches deep by 30 to 34 inches high.

Sinks: Kitchen sinks are usually 33 to 48 inches wide by 22 inches deep; bathroom sinks measure about 16 to 26 inches wide by about 16 to 20 inches deep.

Ranges: Standard stoves are 30 inches wide by about 27 to 30 inches deep by about 35 to 39 inches high. Apartment-size stoves are 24 inches wide; gourmet ranges with double ovens and extra burners can be up to 60 inches wide.

Cook tops: Most are 30 to 48 inches wide by 21 to 26 inches deep.

Refrigerators: Usually about 28 to 36 inches wide by about 32 to 34 inches deep by about 60 to 72 inches high. Built-in refrigerators and those with double doors, bottom freezers, and special features tend to be larger.

Dishwashers: Most are 24 inches wide by 34 inches high.

Washers and dryers: The standard is 27 to 30 inches wide by 27 to 30 inches deep by about 34 to 36 inches high (plus control panels); stacking models and apartment-sized units are narrower.

CHAPTER 3

By Design

When a home inspector examines a property or when a bank
assessor evaluates it, they focus on technical matters—electrical
and plumbing systems, square footage, and the condition of
the roof and foundation. But more often than not, what
prompts us to buy a home is its appearance. Realtors tout the
importance of curb appeal, meaning the first impression a
property presents even before you go inside. We may not be

able to put a dollar value on aesthetics, yet we're profoundly influenced by the way a house looks and feels. Whether you are making improvements to increase your home's marketability or to enhance your own lifestyle, keep beauty in mind as well as function. This chapter offers information and ideas to help you put the best face on your living space.

A House of a Different Color

One of the quickest, easiest, and least expensive ways to improve your home is to paint it. In 1988, I bought a 120-year-old Cape in Gloucester, Massachusetts, that had been completely painted off-white, inside and out. Apparently, the previous owners believed in being nondescript. My then-husband and I disagreed and promptly set about remedying the situation.

Before we'd finished painting the exterior teal, coral, and khaki, scores of passersby had stopped to offer compliments and ask for the paint numbers so they could duplicate our color scheme. *The Boston Globe's* Sunday magazine did a feature article about painting houses, inspired by ours. *The Gloucester Daily Times* photographed our house and ran the full-color picture on the newspaper's front page. Even a Japanese magazine published photos of our house in a travel article. By applying distinctive colors, we emphasized the house's lovely trim and details, integrated it into the landscape, and transformed it from bland to beautiful.

You, too, can use color to emphasize your home's strong points and downplay its deficiencies. Find ten minutes out of your day to flip through a home design magazine and pick a contrasting color scheme that you could use to highlight a positive feature of your home, such as decorative trim. **Remember that dark colors and flat paint minimize imperfections. Light colors tend to make a small building look larger. Unusual hues distinguish your home in a neighborhood of similar structures.**

But color does more than improve appearances. Studies show that color affects us psychologically and physically. Bright, warm colors—red, orange, and yellow—stimulate us and actually raise body temperature and heart rate slightly. Surrounding ourselves with cool hues—green and blue—has the opposite effect. Yellow reminds us of the sun, inspiring optimism and creativity. Pink and peach make us feel more sociable and affectionate—some prisons have been able to reduce incidents of violence by painting inmates' cells pink. Indigo promotes contemplation and serenity. Earth colors (gray, tan, and brown) encourage stability and help to ground us.

Keep these color correspondences in mind as you choose a palette for your home. Pink, peach, and yellow, for example, are good choices for a living or dining room. Blue, green, and indigo are ideal for bedrooms. Orange works well in active areas, such as an exercise room, while mushroom or dove gray might be more suitable for a home office. Darker shades give an impression of elegance and seriousness; pale ones convey congeniality.

Think, too, about your home's location. Blue and green, the colors of water and plants, can make a sunny, southwest space seem more cool and refreshing. Bright hues can warm up a cold, dark, north-facing room. If you live in Manhattan, crisp, clear, sophisticated color combinations—or maybe stark black and white—might appeal to you. Miami, however, invites vibrant splashes of color, such as turquoise and fuchsia. When I lived on the ocean in New England, I chose deep blues and greens for my decorating scheme—colors that reflected my surroundings. When I moved to Texas, I found myself drawn to terracotta, sand, and golden brown.

Consider your site. Do you want your home to stand out or blend in? Peach or yellow brightens a shady plot; gray or sage green nestles neatly into a rocky landscape. A professional florist and gardener I know, whose yard is awash in brilliant flowers, chose to paint her house dark green so it wouldn't detract from her plants. Take your neighbors into account as well. If the house next door is Colonial blue, painting your house dull red could be a nice complement. Of course, if you live in an antique home in an historic district, it's a good idea to stick with colors that are appropriate to its style and time period.

Combining Colors

Although we combine colors every day when we dress, many of us find the prospect of choosing a color scheme for our homes a bit more challenging—perhaps because we don't do it very often or because the scale is so much grander. As a result, most people play it safe and tend to be too conservative with color. Working with color is a lot like cooking—the trick is to blend the right ingredients in the right proportions. If you follow certain tried-and-true "recipes," you'll achieve pleasing results, whether you're choosing a paint color for the exterior of your home, giving your kitchen a minimakeover, or adjusting the furnishings in your living room.

One indispensable tool used by graphic artists, interior designers, and other professionals who work with color was devised by Sir Isaac Newton. Known as the "color wheel," it takes the band of seven hues found in a rainbow and bends it to form a circle. M.E. Chevreul, the French colorist whose theories influenced the Impressionist painters, developed a series of color harmonies or inherently pleasing color combinations,

based on this wheel. For a visual reference, go to
http://en.wikipedia.org/wiki/Color_wheel. Using the color
wheel and the color tips that follow, select a color combination
you can use to highlight a room or feature of your home.

TRIED-AND-TRUE COLOR SCHEMES

Analogous: A combination that incorporates three colors
that fall side-by-side on the color wheel, such as blue,
turquoise, and green.

Complementary: A color scheme comprised of two colors
that oppose one another on the color wheel—green and
red, blue and orange, or purple and yellow.

Split-complementary: An arrangement that combines a color
plus the hues that fall on either side of its complement on
the wheel, for instance, yellow plus fuchsia and indigo.

Monochromatic: A color scheme that uses a single color in
various shades and tones, such as beige mixed with taupe,
cream, and khaki, or orange combined with peach, russet,
and coral.

TEN TIPS FOR CHOOSING
A GREAT COLOR SCHEME

1. Think of your home as your stage. What colors express your personality best? Shy, sensitive people might feel comfortable with neutrals, pastels, or cool colors; dynamic individuals may prefer a bright palette.

2. Let the great masters inspire you. Look at how your favorite artist uses color in a painting you like and incorporate the same colors into your plan. Follow Maxfield Parrish's lead, for instance, and combine the peacock blue and salmon he often used in his paintings to create a striking complementary color scheme.

3. Use a patterned scarf, tie, or shirt as a guide. Transfer the colors combined on the fabric to your home.

4. Choose three colors and combine them in these percentages: 60 percent of the main color, 30 percent of a second color, and 10 percent of an accent color. For example, paint the sides of your house Colonial blue,

paint the trim ecru, and paint the doors and window grilles barn red.

5. To promote harmony use the same color scheme throughout your home, or use a single theme color with slight variations in different rooms.

6. Don't be afraid to use bold colors. Most people avoid strong, bright colors because they think they'll grow tired of them, but if you really love a color it will make you feel good every time you look at it.

7. Take paint, fabric, carpet, and wallpaper samples home; they may look different in the store than in your own environment.

8. Look at colors in different types of lighting (natural and artificial) and at different times of the day. Various light situations will affect the way you see colors.

9. Choose a shade darker than you think you'll like for the exterior of your home. Bright sunlight makes colors look lighter than they seem on paint swatches.

10. Don't be swayed by trends. In the home industry, color palettes change almost as rapidly as they do in the fashion world, but you probably won't redecorate as often as you update your wardrobe. Choose colors for your home that you enjoy and with which you will continue to feel comfortable year after year.

Let There Be Light

Electric lighting is humankind's attempt to imitate the sun and to extend daytime. In our homes, we can attempt to replicate the way Nature lights up our world to create inherently pleasing interior environments. Sometimes the sun shines down on us in brilliant beams; other times it peeks from behind clouds. In the forest, sunlight filters through leaves and branches, dappling the ground with light and shadows. At night, the moon's soft illumination casts a cool, mysterious glow. Strive for this same versatility when you select lighting for your home.

Spend a ten-minute session designing a new lighting plan for one section of your home. Consider the many ways your space is likely to be used and the various kinds of lighting described below. In your master bathroom, for instance, you'll probably want bright lighting over the sink for shaving and applying makeup, but you might prefer to illuminate the area around your soaking tub with a soft, relaxing glow. **You don't have to settle for a single light source, such as the standard overhead fixture above the dining room table. Instead, install various types of lighting that will fulfill all your needs.**

INTERIOR LIGHTING CATEGORIES

Ambient lighting refers to the overall, general illumination in a room. Often this is provided by one or more ceiling fixtures.

Task lighting is usually bright and positioned in a specific spot for a specific purpose. Reading lamps in a living room, track lights directed on a kitchen counter, and fixtures above the bathroom sink fall into this category.

Mood lighting is generally soft and indirect, intended to create a peaceful or romantic atmosphere. Torchieres and wall sconces can be used to produce mood lighting. Dimmer switches can transform overhead fixtures and table lamps into mood lighting, too.

Accent lighting emphasizes an area or object, such as a spotlight directed on a painting or an illuminated curio cabinet.

You'll also want to consider the various types of artificial lighting that are available to determine which will best serve your needs. A short trip to your local lighting store will reveal a plethora of possibilities—pendants, sconces, canisters, torchieres, brackets, track lights, and more. Each has advantages and limitations, which make it more suitable to some applications than others.

Incandescent lighting is familiar to most of us as the ordinary bulbs in table lamps. Versatile incandescent bulbs can be used in most interior or exterior light fixtures. They emphasize the warm end of the color spectrum and produce a pleasing, rosy-golden light, which makes them the most popular choice for homes and social environments.

Fluorescent lighting became popular because it's more energy efficient than incandescent bulbs. Early fluorescent tubes buzzed and emitted a fuzzy bluish-green glow that was unflattering to most skin tones. Today's improved bulbs offer better color rendition and clarity for home and commercial applications.

Halogen lighting is a relative newcomer in the field and gaining ground. Small, low-wattage bulbs fit neatly into tight places —pendants, tracks, under-kitchen cabinet strips—and produce bright, clear, focused light for accents or special tasks.

Full-spectrum lighting includes the complete color spectrum contained in natural sunlight. As a result, it can be beneficial for the estimated 35 million Americans who experience seasonal affective disorder (a common type of depression that is connected with the annual reduction of sunlight in northern latitudes). Because full-spectrum lighting is closer to natural sunlight, it also renders color more accurately than other types of artificial light, and many art museums use it for this reason.

Solar lighting does away with electrical wiring and energy costs altogether. Ideal for exterior applications, sun-powered lamps can be used to illuminate driveways and walkways, patios, porches, and pool areas.

A Recipe for Kitchen Design

The kitchen is the heart of the home. Friends and family members gather in the kitchen, not just to eat but to socialize as well. Parties may start in the living room, but they frequently end up in the kitchen. The kitchen is also a major factor when you're buying or selling a home. Most experts agree that updating your kitchen is one of the best investments you can make in your property and will increase its value more than just about any other home improvement. However, **if you are upgrading your kitchen with the goal of enhancing your home's marketability, don't invest more than 10 to 15 percent of your home's selling price.**

Most likely, you already have a sense of the feeling you wish to achieve—casual and comfortable, sleek and sophisticated, or elegant and elaborate. To some extent, the style/period of your home will influence how you design your kitchen, although I've seen ultra-modern kitchens that blended perfectly into mid-nineteenth century loft condos. (Of course, few of us would be content with a truly authentic antique kitchen, *sans* electricity and indoor plumbing!)

The best way to get started on kitchen improvements is to evaluate how you want your kitchen space to be used. Take ten minutes to divide the current space into zones—areas for food preparation, cooking, cleanup, and storage. Use paper if you're having a hard time visualizing. You may also decide to include additional zones for entertaining, laundry, etc. See if there are any appliances or moveable items that need to be relocated to a more appropriate zone. If so, move them.

Something Old, Something New

Few homeowners today take a purist approach; it's more interesting to be eclectic. Antique houses, for example, almost always sport up-to-date bathrooms and kitchens. Contemporary dwellings often acknowledge the past in their designs. When my yoga teacher built his present meditation retreat, he included Depression-era windows taken from a house he'd owned previously, along with some stained glass beauties that had been rescued from an old church.

Don't feel you must be a slave to a particular style. Mix and match old elements with new ones and pair unique styles. An antique dealer I know believes every home, regardless of its age or design, should include at least one thing that's Chinese. I have incorporated an Arts and Crafts pediment, an Art Nouveau converted gas ceiling light, a three-hundred-year-old Country French dining table, and a contemporary Italian leather sofa into my 1980 Texas ranch house, and they look just as good here as they did in my 1860s New England Cape.

The next time you drive by a salvage yard, flea market, or antique shop, pull over and hunt for vintage architectural finds, such as mantels, columns, moldings, claw-foot tubs, and old doors to complement your home.

Shopping Tips

Shopping for home furnishings, appliances, and materials can be a daunting experience as the choices are practically unlimited. It's easy to get intimidated when you consider the cost of these purchases and the fact that you'll have to live with your decisions for a long time. Here are some dos and don'ts to help make the process easier.

- Do your homework online or via catalogs and magazines before you shop. (*Consumer Reports* and organizations such as AARP provide guidelines and information about products—check them out, too.)
- Do plan ahead—remember, special orders can take up to three months to arrive.
- Do take your floor plan, elevations, and binder/file of pictures with you whenever you shop.
- Do take manufacturers' samples of paint, fabric, carpet, wallpaper, etc. home so you can see them in your own environment.

- Do take along samples of paint, fabric, carpet, wallpaper, etc. that you already have in your home and would like to coordinate with new items.
- Do take a measuring tape with you.
- Do shop with a partner or other person who is a principal decision-maker.
- Do call ahead and make an appointment with a design consultant, if necessary.
- Don't shop when you're tired.
- Don't take the kids shopping with you.
- Don't take along friends or relatives unless they are essential to the decision-making process; their opinions may influence you unduly.
- Don't hesitate to haggle over prices. Some stores will negotiate, some won't, but it's always worth a try.
- Don't attempt to do everything at once. Break the process down into a number of targeted shopping trips and quit when your head starts spinning.

One last suggestion: Take plenty of photos—before, during, and after—to chronicle your progress. You'll want to have a record of your adventure and be able to share the experience with family and friends.

PART TWO

The Tips

CHAPTER 4

Lawn and Landscape

See your yard as others see it.

That woodpile in the back may be convenient, but others may view it as an eyesore. Ditto the rusting swing set, kids' toys strewn about the yard, moldering lawn chairs, exposed trash cans, sagging fence, and collection of plastic bird feeders with squirrel guards. Especially if you're selling your house, go outside right now and spend ten minutes really looking at your yard with fresh eyes—the way a stranger would see it. Note eyesores on a sheet of paper. Maybe that garden gnome with the chipped face isn't as cute as you once thought he was. The trellis looked great when you put it up ten years ago, but now it's falling apart. What would you do differently? Note that as well—then prioritize your improvements. This may be the best ten minutes you've ever spent!

Don't take on too much.

Start small and remember the virtues of low-maintenance. Begin with the areas of your yard that show the most (usually the ones facing the street). If you have no trouble keeping these small areas looking good, gradually expand each year. Hint: Always ask yourself if you're enjoying what you're doing.

Graph your garden.

Before you set out to rejuvenate your garden, sketch a plan of the garden to scale. Watch how the sun tracks across the area and draw lines to indicate patterns of sun and shade. Note on the plan whatever plants you intend to put in. Because the sun's position will change and plants will blossom or die back at different times of the year, it's a good idea to make several drawings—at least one for each month of the growing season.

Get your soil analyzed.
Before you plant flowers, shrubs, or vegetables, get your soil analyzed for alkaline/acidity, certain toxic materials or heavy metals, and other factors. Take a sample of your soil to the county extension service, and they'll run a complete analysis for you, for a minimal fee.

Consider adding a decorative fence.
If your home is near a street or sidewalk, putting up a fence could provide the valuable illusion of privacy and safety. In most cases, a wooden picket, split-rail, or decorative wrought iron fence that's about chest-high is best. They define your personal space without appearing forbidding. Hurricane and

stockade fences can make your home seem like a walled fortress.

 PRODUCT PICK

Decorative wrought iron fences, like those intricate beauties that graced Victorian homes, are expensive and require upkeep. The EverIron Ornamental Polymer Fence from GeoMatrix, made of black polymer, is easy to install and maintenance-free. Period details and one-piece construction make this handsome imitation a practical choice.

Plant climbing flowers along a fence.

Even pretty white picket fences imply "no trespassing." To make your yard appear warm and inviting, plant climbing flowers or vines along a fence.

FOR SALE SHOW & SELL

If you're showing your house between late fall and spring in an area where plants die back during the winter, don't put trellises with herbaceous vines or plant annuals around the house. A trellis with dead vines will just look messy. Instead, add a structure that will remain attractive and visible all year: A garden bench, arbor, or statue are all eye-pleasing options. If you're showing your home in late spring through early fall, plant a cheerful show of bulbs (spring), flowering shrubs and vines (summer), or annuals (summer/fall) around the foundation of your home to add that perfect color accent. Keep all plantings, trees, and shrubs around your home neatly trimmed so they appeal to passersby or prospective buyers.

Add a window box.

Decorative window boxes planted with flowers add a colorful touch to any home. Paint window boxes to match your window trim or front door, then fill them with easy-care annuals that will bloom all season. Coleus, impatiens, and begonias grow well in semi-shade; nasturtiums, petunias, pansies, and geraniums add a cheerful appearance in a sunny spot. Hint: Window boxes need watering frequently—up to twice a day in very hot, dry weather. Don't plant them if you don't think you'll water them.

Plant a flowering hedge.

Robert Frost wrote, "Good fences make good neighbors," but a flowering hedge could be an even better way to define your boundaries. Handsome, flowering shrubs accentuate your neighbor's yard as well as your own. Depending on your site, consider planting forsythia, azalea, wisteria, rosemary, lavender, viburnum, hydrangea, or privet to separate your property from your neighbor's.

Attract birds.

Birds like shrubs and trees that produce berries and fruit. Plant chokecherry, elderberry, crab apple, or mulberry to attract birds. Sunflowers will also tempt feathered friends to visit your home.

Attract butterflies.

Butterfly weed and butterfly bush are logical choices if you want to attract butterflies. Butterflies are also drawn to plants that offer broad, flat landing pads, such as Mexican sage, lantana, black-eyed Susan, coneflower, daisies, asters, cosmos, coreopsis, calendulas, crimson clover, and verbena.

Attract hummingbirds.

Plant red, tube-shaped flowers—columbine, monarda (bee balm), larkspur, penstemon, lupine, nasturtium, and nicotiana (flowering tobacco)—to attract hummingbirds to your garden.

Add an arbor.

Warm up your yard with the addition of an arbor. Plant hardy, climbing vines that will wind around the arbor and provide beauty as well as shade. Fragrant wisteria is a particularly good choice. Or you could plant grapevines and enjoy the fruit of your labors, literally.

Consider laying stone over an old concrete slab.

If your concrete patio, basketball court, or driveway needs a facelift, consider purchasing handsome flagstone slabs in varying sizes to overlay on the old foundation.

Disguise an old concrete slab.

Concrete stain transforms drab, gray concrete into a field of color. Concrete acid stain creates a rich medley of hues to resemble marble, stone, or an artist's canvas. This is a great way to update old patios, sidewalks, and basketball courts.

Consider resurfacing your concrete sidewalk.

Want to give a boring concrete sidewalk a pretty new face? Consider resurfacing it with brick veneer. Hint: If you do go this route, lay out the design first on the dry sidewalk, to make sure you like it, before you position the brick permanently in mortar.

Clear the walk.

Make sure the walkway to your home is inviting. Level any uneven pavers and consider upgrading to something more attractive (slate, brick, concrete "stones," etc.) if your current walkway is an eyesore. Make sure the path is wide enough to walk on comfortably and doesn't flood or get muddy when it rains. Keep grass, weeds, leaves, and other debris cleared off.

Plant a decorative border along a sidewalk.

Spotlight your sidewalk by planting a border of low-growing groundcover on either side. This provides a transition zone into your yard. Hint: Choose durable plants that can withstand some foot traffic. Myrtle and ivy are good choices.

FAST FIX

Give your yard a nostalgic touch. Position a decorative bench, reminiscent of those found in city parks, under a shady tree in your yard. Or hang a porch swing from the branch of an old oak tree.

Add inviting seating.

If your yard is large enough, you can create clusters of seats with a table or other amenities, or design several seating areas. Take advantage of a view: Site your bench or other seating so it looks at something pleasant—your house, garden, or an inviting distant view. Container plantings will add color and charm, as long as they're the same scale and style as the seating. Make sure the seating is in keeping with the style of your home and landscape. A formal group of benches would overpower a tiny yard or seem incongruous with a casual cabin.

Follow your nose.

Choose fragrant blooms for your flower gardens—lilacs, purple petunias, hyacinths, lavender, lily of the valley—to perfume the air with delicious aromas. Hint: Don't plant heavily scented flowers near a patio, deck, or other outdoor seating area; your serene retreat will become a bee haven.

Plant ornamental grasses.

Low-maintenance ornamental grasses offer an attractive alternative to formal flower beds and shrubs. Tall varieties can also serve as screens to provide privacy or define your property's boundaries.

Plant a decorative ground cover in your yard.

Here's another easy-care alternative to the standard grassy lawn—ground covers such as myrtle, ivy, sedum, and vinca require little care, just some periodic trimming to keep them in line. Ground covers also add texture and color to your property, breaking up a uniform blanket of kelly-green turf.

Create a tropical paradise.

Why settle for the usual boring annuals that every garden center sells in six-packs? Instead, borrow a leaf from garden designers' notebooks and grow trendy tropicals. Cannas, elephant ears, ipomoea vines, flowering sages, coleus, dahlias, and many other tropical beauties will add an exotic touch to your garden beds and make it clear that you're up with the latest gardening trends. If you haven't seen some of the new, show-stopping varieties of old-time plants like cannas, coleus, and dahlias, check out the selections at better garden centers and plant catalogs and be prepared to do a double-take. These are not your grandmother's plants!

Throw your yard a curve.

Gently winding curves add a graceful touch in a yard. Consider adding a low curved wall, curved flowerbeds, an S-shaped sidewalk, or rounded terraces.

Position a handsome statue in a flower bed as a focal point. A statue of the Buddha or Kwan Yin is considered lucky in feng shui.

Hide your foundation.

If the foundation detracts from your home's appearance, hide it with an attractive ground cover that stays green year-round. Ivy, portulacaria, and sedum are good choices for camouflaging a low foundation. To add color and textural variety, grow perennials like hardy ferns, bleeding hearts, hellebores, and hostas in shady areas. Peonies, Siberian iris, and daylilies are great in sunny ones. Add bulbs—daffodils, crocus, hyacinths, tulips, and snowdrops—for early-spring interest. If your foundation is high enough, consider covering it with hardy boxwood or holly—but be diligent about keeping these shrubs trimmed. Yucca and rosemary work well in hot, dry climates.

Take the edge off.

Plant shrubs at the corners of your house to soften those hard lines. Twining vines on trellises will do the trick, too.

Plant an herb garden.

In Colonial times, herb gardens were a standard feature outside many kitchens. There's no reason why today's home owners can't also enjoy having fresh herbs at their fingertips. Lots of herbs are easy to grow and don't require much space. Some, such as rosemary and chives, blossom with pretty flowers or perfume the air with a delightful scent.

FOR SALE SHOW & SELL

Trim shrubs, pull weeds, and rake leaves to keep your yard looking its best at all times.

Add color with foliage.

Here's a great landscaping trick for people who want a lot of garden color without having to worry about when things will be in bloom. Use foliage to add landscape color. By putting plants with colorful foliage, like coleus, heucheras, hostas, cannas, and some of the new foliage geraniums, in containers and garden beds, you'll be guaranteed season-long color (as long as you remember to water). Then you can enjoy your flowers as extras.

Enjoy some enchanted evenings.

If you like to sit outside on warm nights, choose flowers that bloom in the evening. Annuals like moonflowers, some water lilies, nicotiana (flowering tobacco), four o'clocks, and of course, the fabled night-blooming cereus and angel's trumpet (brugmansia) are just a few you might want to consider. Plants with white or yellow flowers give off a soft glow as the sun sets. Plants with gray or silver foliage, like dusty miller, artemisia, and lamb's ears, also show up well. If you live in the Southeast, you can add flowering jessamine and gardenias to your plant palette.

Outfox the deer.

Hungry deer have become an increasing problem for homeowners across the United States. Without an eight-foot fence (at
least) and some electric wires around the perimeter of your
property, it's often open season on your plants. The solution?
Plant things they won't eat. Daffodils, ornamental grasses, and
thorny plants rank high on the list of foods deer generally
avoid. Make your landscape challenging for them, and they'll
head for the smorgasbord next door instead. Hint: Many garden
centers and county agricultural extension services can provide
lists of deer-resistant plants that will grow well in your area.

Create a rock garden.

If you're a reluctant gardener or live in an inhospitable climate
where it's difficult to grow flowers, design a rock garden
instead. Put down a bed of small stones a few inches
deep—round, brownish-gray river stones look more natural
than standard driveway gravel. Then position larger, inter-
estingly shaped rocks at various points as decorative accents.

When you have more time to spare, you can also incorporate statuary, a bird bath, solar-powered lamps, or a few easy-care plants in containers into your design. Designate it as a quiet spot for rest and reflection and include a bench or a couple chairs where you can sit and enjoy your masterpiece.

Design a labyrinth.

Centuries ago, labyrinths were built on sacred sites throughout Europe and in other parts of the world. Not to be confused with mazes, these circular designs are making a comeback today; many people enjoy walking them as a form of meditation and relaxation. You can fashion your own labyrinth from stones (like the rock garden described at left), defining the pathways or "circuits" with larger stones laid on top of the small ones or create a "turf" labyrinth by cutting the pathways into the grass. Another option is to plant small shrubs or flowers in winding rows to designate the circuits.

Here's an easy way to keep weeds from invading your stone or brick patio. Early each spring, scatter rock salt (the same kind used to melt snow and ice) over the stone or brick. The salt will soak into the ground and kill the weeds. Usually once a year is enough, but depending on your locale, you may need to repeat the salting process a second time during the growing season.

Switch to organic fertilizer.

Instead of loading up your land with toxic chemical fertilizers, go organic. Bone meal, compost, cottonseed meal, mulch, and manure are safe for kids, pets, and the environment.

Get rid of dandelions, naturally.

Corn gluten meal is a natural herbicide that helps keep dandelions from proliferating in your lawn. It's effective for limiting other weeds, too. Spread it on your lawn in early spring before weeds sprout. Best of all, it's safe for kids, pets, and the environment.

FAST FIX

Try a global perspective. Here's a "what's old is new again" trend: gazing balls (also called gazing globes), those reflecting balls that are usually set up on stands. Garden designers love them because they add light, color, and an exotic touch to any landscape. Instead of breakable glass, you can buy stainless steel or copper gazing balls and leave them out all year round. Some catalogs carry solar gazing balls in swirly patterns that absorb light and release it at night. Gazing balls come in many sizes and colors, from silver and gold to luminous rainbow hues. Set them on stands, float them in water gardens, or nestle them under foliage in your garden beds. The possibilities are endless—have fun!

Light up the night.

Light the way to your home with easy-to-install solar-powered lights. Simply stick these inexpensive, energy-saving devices into the ground along the edge of your driveway or sidewalk—no electric wiring or batteries needed.

Protect a concrete driveway.

Invest in some concrete sealer to prevent oil drips from staining your concrete driveway.

Patch an asphalt driveway.

Fill cracks, chinks, and small holes in an asphalt driveway with asphalt pitch (a mixture of coal tar, sand, clay, and water). Trowel the mixture into the breaks in the pavement, then sprinkle sand on the pitch. Drive over the patch to press it firmly into place and let it dry overnight.

FAST FIX

In just a few years, weeds can cause cracks and destroy a paved driveway. Don't let them get a foothold. If you aren't against using chemicals, you can extend the life of your driveway by spraying the invaders with a little weed killer as soon as you notice them poking through the pavement.

Reduce soil erosion.

Keep your property from washing away. Hire someone (or set aside a day on your calendar) to build terraces in your yard to slow down water runoff and reduce soil erosion. Planting native grasses, ground covers, and hardy shrubs will help to hold the soil together, too.

Just add water.

Whether it's a serene water garden with flowering water lilies, lotus, and huge, colorful koi, or a simple birdbath, a water feature can really enhance your property. Bubblers and solar fountains make small water gardens and recirculating fountains and streams easy to operate. Or invest in the latest landscape trend—a recirculating water feature that seems to disappear into a bed of rocks like a mystical spring.

Garden in a barrel.

Barrel gardens let you place a decorative water feature close to your deck or porch. Fill a large oak barrel with water, then add goldfish and smaller water plants, such as papyrus and water hyacinths.

Consider creating a dry stream.

If you live in an arid locale, one way to increase yard appeal is to carve out a dry stream and fill it with stones and gravel. Some people add to the effect by planting ferns and money-wort along the sides, so the foliage hangs over the banks. You might even want to add a little footbridge crossing the stream.

Add a birdhouse for purple martins.

Purple martins eat mosquitoes. Invite these helpful birds to hang around your house by putting up a house just for them. They're common throughout the East, South, Midwest, Southwest, and Plains areas.

Bathe the birds.

Invite birds and butterflies to take a bath. Put a standing bird-bath in your yard, or place a few stones in the middle of a pond or stream to give thirsty winged visitors something to land on. A large stone with a scooped out impression can serve as a birdbath, too—simply fill the recessed area with water.

Disguise a septic tank.

Here's an easy and attractive way to hide the opening to your septic tank, yet leave it accessible for pumping and maintenance. Purchase a large, fiberglass or plastic planter from a garden supply store and turn it upside down over the opening. Then lay a circular piece of glass, metal, or plastic on top of the planter to create a table. You can set a decorative plant or lawn ornament on top if you wish.

CHAPTER 5

The View from the Street

Opt to preserve architectural details.

Many older homes feature attractive architectural details such as corner boards, fascia boards, ornate window frames, dental moldings, and other decorative trim. If you opt to replace old wooden clapboard, don't remove or cover up these architectural details. Ask your contractor to save the original features and fit the new siding around them, in order to preserve your home's character.

Don't let dormers ruin your roofline.

Adding a shed dormer can significantly increase the amount of usable space in a house's second story. But don't destroy the original roof line. Start the dormer at least a foot in from the edge of the roof and slope it into the roof's peak. If your home has interesting corner posts or decorative trim, reproduce these features on the shed dormer, too, for consistency.

Avoid faux wood-grain siding.

If you opt to use siding made of vinyl, fiberglass, or another manmade material on your home's exterior, avoid wood-grain patterns. They scream "fake." Real wood clapboard doesn't have a distinctive grain, and when painted it's virtually smooth. Choose siding with a smooth, texture-free surface for a more authentic look.

Research your home's history.

Check your home's "pedigree" before you begin remodeling. It may appear on a local, state, or national historic register or have been designed by a well-known architect. Perhaps your house once belonged to someone notable; George Washington might even have slept there. If the building has architectural or historical significance, you'll want to maintain as much of its original detail and character as possible—like antique furniture and collectible *objets d'art*, a period home is worth more if it's restored, not remodeled.

SHOW & SELL

Even if your home isn't a national treasure, learning about its history could provide you and your realtor with an interesting story to tell prospective buyers. Your home's unique personality could distinguish it from the competition and help you sell it faster.

Check with your town's historic commission before renovating.

If you live in an old city that prizes its antique architecture, you may have to get the approval of the local historic commission before you can undertake exterior renovations. Some communities, such as Salem, Massachusetts, have strict guidelines that specify what's acceptable and what's not. Other towns protect First Period homes (those built before 1725) and buildings with special significance. Find out what rules apply in your area or to your house before you begin work.

Shop for replacement windows.

If your current windows are outdated or need replacing, start shopping for new ones. Make sure the replacement windows you choose are appropriately sized and of a compatible design for your home's style and age. Picture windows, greenhouse windows, and bay/bow window sets, for instance, aren't appropriate for most houses built before 1930. Most eighteenth- and nineteenth-century houses originally featured double-hung windows, usually two-over-two, six-over-six, or nine-over-six, depending on the period and style. You don't have to sacrifice energy efficiency for authenticity—or vice versa. Major window manufacturers offer a wide range of styles and sizes to fit virtually any home. Study historic structures in your area or look at books and magazines devoted to antique restoration before putting new windows in your home.

 PRODUCT PICK

Andersen makes Frank Lloyd Wright–style windows that add a distinctive touch.

Find a way to incorporate stained glass.

Stained glass windows have been prized for their beauty since medieval times. Installing one in your home can serve more than one purpose simultaneously—the rich colors and designs create a beautiful accent, letting in light while masking a less-than-ideal view. Have a stained glass window affixed in place permanently or hang one in its own frame in front of an existing window.

Aim for symmetry when replacing windows.
Most homes look best when all the windows are of the same design. Don't mix double-hung windows with awning or casement styles, for instance.

Align the tops of windows.
Align the tops of the windows to create symmetry. The result is harmonious rather than chaotic.

 PRODUCT PICK

Pella's Vivid View screens made with fine-gauge material let in up to 50 percent more light and provide better ventilation than ordinary screens.

Reglaze windows.

Over time, the glazing compound around a windowpane will dry out and crack. Pick one window to work on for the next ten minutes. Dig out the old glaze and brush-clean the window frames to remove dirt. Squeeze new glaze into your palm and roll it into a long, thin rope. Fit the glaze neatly around the window panes and smooth it with a putty knife, to keep your window airtight and secure.

Break up boring walls.

If you have an expanse of blank, boring, or downright ugly wall with no windows, put up a trellis. You can find many styles, from lattice to wire, in garden centers, garden catalogs, and online. Later, when you have time, add flowers. Make sure you choose a trellis style and flower colors that suit your home's design and color.

Consider the other homes in your neighborhood before painting your house.
When deciding what color to paint your home, take into consideration the other buildings nearby. Choose hues that compliment and coordinate with your neighbors' homes, rather than clashing.

Choose a house paint color that's appropriate for its style.
Each period and architectural style is associated with specific color palettes. When choosing paint colors for your home, consider using colors that are characteristic of its period, style, and locale. For example, Victorian houses, such as San Francisco's "Painted Ladies," originally sported vibrant color combinations. Only a few hues—charcoal, dark red, yellow ochre, gray, and

white—are authentic to seventeenth- and early eighteenth-century Capes and saltboxes. Salmon and turquoise are perfect for Miami's Art Deco bungalows.

Know that color charts can be deceiving.

As a rule, paint samples appear darker on color charts and little squares than they will when used on exterior walls. Remember that sunlight will cause colors to look lighter, and over time, paint will fade. So opt for a darker shade than you initially think is right.

Accentuate decorative architectural details.

If your house boasts distinctive architectural details—moldings, cornices, corner boards, pillars, etc.—emphasize them. Choose a contrasting color for the trim, instead of painting the entire exterior the same hue. Depending on your home's style, you may want to highlight interesting features by using several coordinating colors.

Make a point to paint one side of your house each year.
If you don't have the time or inclination to paint your entire
house all at once, set a date this year to paint one side of it.
Sunlight illuminates each side from a different angle anyway, so
slight variations in color won't be noticed.

Consider adding texture with brick or stone veneer.
Brick or natural stone, sliced thin, can be applied as a veneer to
exterior walls to add visual interest. It's easier and less expensive to update old siding with veneer than with full-size bricks
or stones.

 PRODUCT PICK

Robinson Brick Company offers a line of brick and stone
veneer for exterior or interior use, in lots of interesting
colors and sizes.

Study other houses in your area to get ideas.

Go on a photo safari in your own community or a nearby town to gather ideas. Look at how other people have used colors, landscaped their yards, put on additions, and handled challenges similar to the ones you're addressing. Take pictures. If you see something you really like, ask homeowners for information—paint numbers, product names, what contractor they used, etc. Most people enjoy talking about their home improvements and will share information with you. Remember, imitation is the most sincere form of flattery.

Choose appropriately sized shutters.

Originally, shutters were designed to provide protection from the elements and intruders. Today they function mainly as decorative features. If you like the look of exterior shutters on your windows, remember their original purpose. Don't choose puny louvered panels to nail beside your windows—choose shutters that are appropriately sized and affix them to the window frames, so that if you were to close them they would completely cover your windows.

Choose teak, redwood, or cedar when building a deck.

All three of these handsome woods are good choices for decks and porches (as well as for outdoor furniture). They withstand inclement weather conditions and require little care. Teak, which is often used in boat building, is the most expensive of the three. Don't paint a deck made of teak, redwood, or cedar. The wood ages to a pleasant color over time. Hint: Treating the wood with a sealer, however, will help keep it from warping.

Consider pressure-treated lumber when building a deck.
Pressure-treated lumber has been specially prepared to prevent damage from insects and fungus. You don't have to paint it either. The wood ages over time to a grayish-brown color similar to cedar.

Choose faux wood for your deck.

Imitation redwood or weathered cedar won't fool the discerning eye, but a deck made of compressed wood fiber and plastic composite is durable and virtually maintenance-free.

Consider building a deck over your garage.

If your home sits on a small lot and your garage has a flat roof, consider tapping the unused area atop a garage for a roof top deck. This arrangement works best when a single-story garage adjoins a two-story house.

Remember that variety is the spice of life.

Add variety to a deck by laying out floorboards to create a pattern. Zigzag, herringbone, checkerboard, or diagonal configurations give a deck more visual appeal.

Consider building a multi-leveled deck.

Another way to increase a deck's visual appeal is to vary the levels. If you're planning on adding a deck to your home, consider one with two, three, or more distinct sections, each a few steps higher or lower than the adjoining one. Before committing to a specific design, give careful thought to how each section will be used and how traffic patterns will flow from one level to the next.

Dress up a porch.

Add interest to your porch with a decorative knee wall, a short wall about knee height, instead of an ordinary railing. Create an attractive original design or take one from a book and make a template. Hint: Simple designs, such as those used for stencils or gingerbread trim, usually work best.

Deck out your deck. Colorful hanging baskets can add pizzazz to an ordinary deck. Choose attractive wire-and-coir-liner baskets and fill them with hanging plants that will grow well in your light conditions. Vining nasturtiums, petunias, tuberous begonias, trailing geraniums, creeping zinnias, sweet alyssum, and lobelia are good for sunny spots, ipomoea (ornamental sweet potato) vines, and variegated ivy are better suited to shadier sites.

Consider updating a porch railing.

Old-fashioned iron railings, like those that were popular in the fifties and sixties, give your home a dated appearance. To bring your porch up to speed, you may want to remove the old railings and replace them with something more imaginative.

Check building codes before putting up a railing.

Many communities have building codes that specify how high a railing must be and how much space must be left between the balusters. Before you add a railing on your porch or deck, check to see what regulations apply in your area.

Don't make the garage a focal point.

In many instances, the garage occupies a prominent position in a house's design; it may even be the first thing you notice from the curb. However, the entrance to the car's "home" shouldn't detract from the entrance to your own living space. If you're adding a garage or redesigning the exterior of your home, avoid positioning the garage doors so they face the street; place the entrance to your garage at the side or back of the house instead.

Choose carriage house doors for your garage.

Instead of the usual metal garage doors, add character to your home by choosing wooden carriage house doors or barn doors instead.

Hang carriage lamps on your garage.

Complete the image by hanging old-fashioned carriage lanterns (wired for electricity, of course) to compliment your garage doors. Hint: Choose lamps that seem larger than you think you'll need. They'll look smaller when affixed to your garage than they do in the showroom.

Opt for a curved driveway.

From the perspective of feng shui (the ancient Chinese art of placement) a straight driveway conducts energy too quickly from the street to your home and can produce tension. Instead, select a driveway design that curves gently toward your home, like a meandering stream or forms a "lucky" horseshoe that allows easy entrance and exit. (See my books 10-Minute Feng Shui and 10-Minute Feng Shui Room by Room for more information.)

Display your street address on your mailbox.

Many communities now encourage residents to prominently display the numbers of their street address so emergency services (ambulance, police, fire department) can find your home easily. Visitors to your home, delivery people, etc. will also appreciate it if you attach attractive numerals to your mailbox.

Make a date to clean gutters and downspouts.
Gutters and downspouts only work when they're properly installed and kept clean. Mark a date on your calendar to clear out collected debris so your gutters and downspouts function effectively.

Replace ineffective gutters.
Ineffective gutters allow rainwater to run down the sides of your house, which may damage siding, compromise the foundation, or allow moisture to seep into your basement. If gutters have merely pulled away from fascia boards and/or downspouts, reattach them. If necessary, replace gutters that don't work properly.

Decorate a doghouse to resemble your house.
Replicate your house in miniature for Fido with a little

creativity and matching paint color. Designing your dog's digs to resemble your own creates a sense of symmetry. It's a great conversation starter, too.

Decorate the shed.
Make your shed look as attractive as it is functional. If the shed has windows, decorate them with window boxes filled with colorful flowers. If not, plant flowers around the base of the shed to add some cheer and warmth.

Use latticework to hide an eyesore.
Conceal an HVAC unit, gas tank, or trash cans with an attractive lattice-work screen.

Consider adding a greenhouse.
If you live in a cold climate, a greenhouse lets you enjoy your favorite plants all year round. You can also get a jump on planting a vegetable garden by starting seedlings in a greenhouse. A greenhouse that's attached to the house can provide heat for

your home—install fans to circulate solar heat into your interior. If you do have one built, make sure that at least some of the glass panels are equipped with screens to allow adequate ventilation during warm months.

Reflect heat from your roof.

If you live in a hot climate, choose reflective materials for your roof to cut down on air conditioning costs.

Add folding awnings to your house.

Remember the colorful cloth awnings that graced grandma's house? These practical and attractive accents perk up homes that were built during the first half of the twentieth century. Art world giant Edward Hopper found them so appealing he made them the subject of a popular painting.

CHAPTER 6

Making an Entrance

Prevent accidents on slippery steps.

Use textured paint on outdoor steps to produce a safer surface. Combine exterior floor enamel paint with a non-slip additive, then give stair treads two coats of paint. Hint: Rough up the surface first so the paint will adhere better.

Fix Broken Steps.

Brick or stone steps that have cracked or broken over time pose more than an aesthetic problem. They can be a safety hazard as well. Dig out old mortar, then use a trowel to fill in the gaps with fresh mortar. Replace broken bricks or stones and mount new ones securely.

FAST FIX

For a splash of quick color, set a matching pair of stately containers filled with bright flowers on either side of a front entrance to dress it up in a flash. Aim for a multi-layered effect—a tall plant in the center, lower blooms surrounding it, and trailing vines spilling over the sides. You don't have to spring for terracotta, heavy concrete, or wrought-iron urns; today's plastic and fiberglass containers come in many sophisticated faux formats that really can fool the eye.
Hint: Make sure the plantings coordinate with the colors of your house.

Select French doors for extra light.

Take advantage of a great view and let the light shine into your home: Replace solid doors and/or ordinary windows with attractive French doors. Hint: Plain frames look best on contemporary homes, doors with grilles are better choices for older houses.

Combine privacy with convenience.

Many patio and French doors are available with blinds factory-installed between the inner and outer glass panes. Convenient controls allow you to open and close the blinds easily, and because the blinds are encased in glass you'll never have to dust them.

Choose aluminum or vinyl-clad doors for easy maintenance.

Sliding glass or French exterior doors clad with aluminum or vinyl resist fading and corrosion. They don't need to be painted either. However, your color options will be limited.

Choose wood doors for elegance and authenticity.

Real wood doors add a touch of elegance to any home. Wooden doors are the appropriate choice for older homes, especially those built before vinyl, fiberglass, and other modern materials were available. However, a wooden door will require more maintenance than one constructed of manmade materials.

 PRODUCT PICK

Jeld-Wen's handsome Arts and Crafts style wooden doors, with plain or stained glass windows, are specially treated to resist decay, water, and insect infestation.

Repair sliding glass doors.

If your sliding glass doors don't open easily, you may simply need to tighten the screws in the metal tracks so they don't bind.

Restore a damaged doorjamb.

Is your doorjamb looking a little beat-up? Maybe the movers dinged it carrying in your furniture or the dog has tried to scratch his way in. If the wood is still sound (no dry rot or insect infestation), you may be able to avoid replacing the whole thing. Clean and sand the surface to remove dirt and splinters, then fill in the gouges with wood filler. Later, when the filler has dried, sand it smooth and prime and paint it.

Replace a torn screen.

Not only is a torn screen door unsightly, it's ineffective. Replace it by gently prying off the door spline (the trim piece that holds the screen in place). Then remove the old screen and roll a new piece of screen into place. Tuck the edges of the screen into the grooves around the opening, replace the spline, and trim off the excess screen.

Adjust doors so they open and close easily.

If the screws have stripped the wood so they can no longer be tightened completely, remove the screws and glue toothpicks around the insides of the holes. When the glue has dried, screw the hinges securely back in place.

Apply a little bar soap or petroleum jelly to screws before putting them in place—especially if they'll be exposed to the weather. They'll be easier to remove if you need to later.

Avoid faux wood-grain doors.

Fiberglass doors that have been textured to imitate wood grain usually look fake. If you like the convenience of a fiberglass door, choose one with a smooth surface in a color that suits your home. Notice, the grain doesn't show on a real wood door that's been painted, so the faux texture is a dead giveaway.

Paint the front door.

If you don't want to paint your whole house, paint the front door to give your home a fresh, new look—fast.

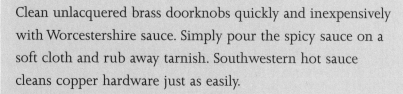

Mount a decorative light fixture.

A distinctive light fixture positioned above or beside the front door gives visitors a good first impression when they come to your home. Choose one that reflects your personality or conveys an image you wish to project.

Light up your life.

Make sure the foyer or front hall of your home is well-lit, not only for safety reasons, but also to give your home an inviting appearance. From the perspective of feng shui, light attracts positive energy called chi. This beneficial chi is considered to be the source of health, wealth, and happiness.

FAST FIX

Fluorescent light bulbs are more energy efficient than incandescents. Save electricity by replacing exterior incandescent bulbs with compact fluorescents.

Attach an attractive doorknob.

Dress up your front door with an attractive doorknob. One of the first things visitors to your home will see and touch, a distinctive doorknob makes a good first impression.

 PRODUCT PICK

Van Dyke's Restorers offers a handsome collection of Arts and Crafts doorknobs, hinges, and other hardware.

Replace old doorknob-and-lock sets that don't function properly. Doorknobs and locks represent security, and if yours don't operate adequately, they'll annoy you every time you enter your home and/or cause you to feel unsafe. Old, worn, or malfunctioning locks may cause prospective buyers to feel uneasy, too. Change them before you put your property on the market.

Consider installing a transom to let in light.

Many mudrooms and back hallways lack windows; consequently, these dark, cramped spaces seem claustrophobic and unfriendly—places to be hurried through as quickly as possible. Make yours more hospitable by having a transom installed above the back door. Even if there's no spot on a wall to put a full window, you'll have room above the door for a transom. A transom window can also be opened to let fresh air flow into a confined, musty room.

FAST FIX

Locks that stick or bind may just need a little oil. Carefully remove the entire knob and lock set, keeping the mechanism intact. If dust and dirt have collected over time, use a hair dryer to blow out particles. Then squirt a little 3-in-One Oil into the mechanism to lubricate the parts. Reattach the lock and doorknob, and operate it a few times until the oil spreads throughout the mechanism.

Hang a wind chime near your door.

The lovely sound of wind chimes invites people to enter your home. According to feng shui, wind chimes also chase away bad vibes and attract good chi—the vital energy that brings health, wealth, and happiness into your life.

Hang a mirror to open up a dark hallway.

If installing a window or transom isn't an option, you can create the effect of space and light by hanging a large mirror on a wall. The mirror imitates a window and produces an illusion of openness. You might even find a mirror with grilles that actually looks like a window.

FAST FIX

Stop looking for your keys and sunglasses. Hang a shelf in your entryway so you have a convenient place to put these things when you come inside. Hint: You can place a small lamp on the shelf, too, to illuminate a dark mudroom or hall.

Choose cheerful colors for your entryway.

Light, bright colors such as yellow, peach, or Granny Smith apple green make a foyer or hallway seem inviting. Because these are the first places guests and household members see when they enter your home, select paint that has a cheery hue. Bright colors will give dark mudrooms or back halls a sense of openness and warmth.

Put lockers in your back hallway.

If household members tend to enter the home through a back hallway or mudroom, add a locker, like those used in gyms, for each member. Lockers keep coats, hats, gloves, boots, etc. neatly organized and hidden from view. Kids can stash backpacks and school materials there, too.

FAST FIX

A wood-framed medicine cabinet with a mirror is an attractive and convenient place to store keys, sunglasses, and other gear you need when you leave the house. Hang one near the entrance you use most often so you don't waste time looking for these essentials. The mirror lets you check your appearance before you go out, too.

Choose durable flooring for an entryway.

Carpet or wood may not be the best choice for an entryway, especially one that kids and pets use frequently. Instead, lay Mexican tile, slate, brick, or vinyl that will stand up to lots of activity. If you tile your entryway, choose a grout color such as gray or brown that will hide dirt.

CHAPTER 7

High-Traffic Areas

Find a way to camouflage wood paneling.
Instead of removing that old-fashioned wood paneling that was
so popular in the fifties and sixties, you could simply apply
textured paint over it. Hint: If you decide to go this route,
prime paneling first so the paint adheres better. Another way to
cover up wood paneling is with wallpaper. Put up lining paper

first for a smooth, even surface, and then apply wallpaper on top of the liner.

 PRODUCT PICK

American Tradition's Texture Paint comes in a variety of colors and several textures to let you create lots of interesting looks—stucco, grass cloth, adobe, and distressed plaster.

Opt for cool colors.

Studies show that we respond physically as well as psychologically to the colors around us. If you live in a hot climate, paint south- and west-facing rooms green, blue, or gray to produce a cooling effect.

Choose warm colors.

If you live in a cold climate, warm up north-facing rooms by painting them peach, yellow, pink, orange, or red.

Use pink, peach, or yellow in the living room.
Colors affect us psychologically, even if we aren't aware of it.
Pink, peach, and yellow inspire sociability, optimism, and
feelings of affection. Consequently, they are good colors to
include in living and family rooms.

Use warm tones in the dining room.
Red, orange, and yellow stimulate appetite, therefore these
colors are good choices for a dining room or kitchen.

Be bold.
Don't be afraid to paint walls bright or dark colors—even in a
small room, choose strong colors to create a dramatic effect.
Worst case scenario, you'll have to repaint.

Paint in order.
When painting a room, be sure to paint the ceiling first and
let it dry before doing the walls. This will prevent pesky drips
and runs.

Dark or bright colors may repel some prospective buyers. You don't have to stick with plain vanilla walls, but neutrals such as sage, taupe, dove gray, or pale amber are better choices than raspberry or espresso.

Let a favorite painting inspire your color scheme.

Can't decide on a color scheme? Let the great masters guide you. Flip through art books until you find a painting you like and examine the way the artist has combined colors in his/her composition. Van Gogh's "Starry Night," for example, emphasizes blues and indigos, with smaller amounts of buttery yellow and mustard. Follow the artist's lead and use the same color palette for your walls, carpeting, upholstery, and accessories.

Select three hues for your color scheme.

A tried-and-true formula for creating successful color schemes uses three different hues in the following proportions: 60 percent of the main color, 30 percent of the second color, and 10 percent of an accent color. (See Chapter 3 for more information.)

Pick an accent color for woodwork.

Instead of the customary off-white woodwork, choose a distinctive color for the trim in your room—especially if you're blessed with decorative crown moldings, wainscoting, dental moldings, or other interesting details. Try peach woodwork with taupe walls or dark green trim with creamy yellow walls.

Pick two tones for your windows.

You can easily accentuate windows by painting the surrounding frames one color and the sash/grille another color. You can also do the same thing with doors—choose one color for the frame/jamb and another for the door itself.

Resurface cracked or damaged walls.

Use textured paint on walls to conceal cracks and other minor damage.

Choose to sponge-paint your walls.

Sponging is one of the easiest and fastest of all decorative painting techniques. The unique, textured look hides minor imperfections in walls and adds drama to your room.

Remember to leave a little room at the top.

You'll get a cleaner-looking line and avoid getting paint on the ceiling if you leave about $1/8$ to $1/4$ inch at the top of the walls instead of painting all the way up to where they join the ceiling. You can do this only if the old color is close to the ceiling color, for instance, white over off-white walls. If you're doing blue over red it won't work very well.

Choose flat paint when hiding imperfections.

Flat paint does a better job of concealing minor imperfections on walls and woodwork. The glossier the paint, the more those little irregularities will stand out.

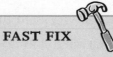
Use paste on prepasted wallpaper.

Prepasted wallpaper is supposed to be easier and less messy to hang, but that's not always the case. Wetting the wallpaper to soften the glue causes some papers to stretch, which can make it harder to hang them straight. Wallpaper paste also provides a stronger bond, especially in bathrooms where moisture can cause paper to peel.

Plan on painting walls before applying wallpaper.

Changes in temperature and humidity can cause wallpaper to shrink ever-so-slightly—just enough to produce hairline separations between panels. Especially if you're hanging dark or bright wallpaper, it's a good idea to first paint your walls the same color as the paper so you won't notice the gaps at the seams.

Purchase all the wall covering at one time.

To make certain your wallpaper matches, purchase all you'll need for the job at the same time. Check dye lot numbers, too, and be sure every roll of paper comes from the same lot. Different dye lots will vary slightly in color and may not match. Hint: Buy a few extra rolls in case you need to replace some at a later date.

Consider granite wall coverings.

Wall coverings made with chips of granite, mica, and vermiculate add a touch of elegance to a wall. The rich texture hides surface imperfections, too.

PRODUCT PICK

Granite wall coverings from Phillip Jeffries Ltd. can be applied to a hollow-core interior door to create a "granite" tabletop. Or cover a piece of $3/4$-inch wallboard to simulate a granite ledge or mantelpiece. You can even wrap this material around columns.

Test a color before you commit to it.

Some paint companies sell small cans of paint so you can test it. Paint a section of your wall and see if you like it, before you paint a whole room.

 PRODUCT PICK

Benjamin Moore offers 2-ounce trial size cans of paint in 260 different colors. Each can of Color Samples contains enough to cover a 2-by-2-foot square of wall.

Fix windows that won't open.

Windows that have become stuck shut can be made operable again with a putty knife. Position the blade between the sash and the window frame, then tap the handle with a hammer to break through accumulated old paint or grime. Open the window and grease the tracks with petroleum jelly.

 PRODUCT PICK

For easy window décor selection, American Blinds, Wallpaper & More offers a sample kit that shows the different blinds, shutters, and louvers in their collection.

Expose a brick chimney.

In many older homes the chimney has been covered up with wallboard, plaster, or paneling. Hire someone to remove it. Old brick adds character to a room; expose it all the way up to the ceiling.

Repair cracks in mortar.

If cracks have developed in the mortar in your fireplace, fix them by first scraping out the old mortar. Use a trowel to fill in the cracks with new mortar, then wipe off excess.

Consider installing a flue liner in your fireplace.

Some old chimneys may require too much work and money to fix, but that doesn't mean your fireplace is useless. One way to ferry smoke and sparks up the chimney safely is to install a flue liner.

FAST FIX

Over time, smoke can build up on the front your fireplace and discolor masonry. Clean bricks or stone by spraying creosote remover on the masonry and scrubbing it with a stiff brush. Wipe off soot and grime with a damp cloth. Repeat if necessary.

Choose a distinctive mantel.

Transform an ordinary fireplace into a dramatic focal point by adding a distinctive mantel. A mantelpiece made of marble or carved mahogany dresses up a traditional room. A hefty slab of mesquite, cedar, or oak adds a striking note to a rustic fieldstone fireplace. A simple shelf of granite or smoky glass makes a smart statement in a contemporary setting.

Consider tiling around a fireplace opening.

Decorative tile is a great tool for dressing up a fireplace. Consider affixing handsome, fireproof ceramic tile to the masonry on the front of the fireplace's opening to give it a distinctive look and to cover minor cracks or other damage.

Purchase a propane or electric stove.

Inspire the charm of an old-fashioned cast-iron wood stove without the inconvenience. Invest in a heating stove fired by propane or electricity that will burn clean and efficiently. A thermostat regulates heat to provide steady, cozy warmth; a blower circulates heat throughout the room.

Consider the option of cast-iron baseboard heating.

Like old-fashioned cast-iron radiators, updated cast-iron baseboards continue to radiate heat into your rooms after the heating unit has shut down. If you're installing a forced hot water heating system in your home, consider this energy-saving option.

 PRODUCT PICK

Century Architectural Specialties recreates a variety of "Old World" trim options—moldings, brackets, etc.—from easy-care fiberglass and polyurethane.

Consider adding a chair rail.

Dining room walls come to life when you add a decorative wooden chair rail. The railing not only protects paint or wallpaper, it divides the walls into upper and lower sections to create extra interest. You could paint the upper portion and wallpaper the lower half, or hang bead board wainscoting below the chair rail and wallpaper the upper wall.

Purchase all the carpeting you need from the same dye lot.
If you want your carpeting to match perfectly, buy it all at the same time from the same dye lot. Carpet from a different dye lot may be slightly different in color. Check the lot numbers to make sure.

Bring carpet samples home.
Before you purchase carpeting, bring samples home so you can see them in your own environment. The lighting in the store probably won't be the same as that in your home. View the samples at various times of the day, in natural and artificial light.

Install a ceiling fan.
A ceiling fan can help reduce both heating and cooling costs by circulating the air in your living space. From the perspective of feng shui (an ancient Chinese practice that lets you change

your life by changing your home), ceiling fans placed in public areas of your home also help to keep your social life from languishing.

Steer clear of hollow-core interior doors.

Hollow-core interior doors, usually made of luan mahogany veneer panels, are an inexpensive option, and they look it. Not only are they totally without character, the thin wooden veneer chips easily and can be broken through without much effort. Opt for solid wooden doors inside your home for durability as well as aesthetics.

Choose paneled doors for older homes.

If your home was built before World War II, flat surface doors probably aren't appropriate. If you replace interior doors, choose simple raised-panel or inset-panel wooden ones instead.

Use metal latches on old doors.

Instead of doorknobs, you may want to use antique metal latches on interior doors in houses built before 1800.

Consider installing French doors to divide rooms.

With French doors, you can create a separation between rooms without the permanence of a wall. When you want to conserve heat or air conditioning, provide privacy, etc., you can shut the doors. Because you can still see through the glass panels, however, a sense of spaciousness remains. Hint: Doors with grilles look better in older homes.

Hang drapery to divide rooms.

Give your home an Old World look by hanging handsome drapery—velvet or tapestry, for instance—between two rooms as a divider. This pretty treatment also has a practical side. Drapery can prevent drafts and keep heat contained in a particular area when hung between a living room and a hall or stairway. When it's not in use, tie back the drape with a pretty tasseled cord.

Buff wooden floors to a soft glow. Once or twice a year, apply a coat of clear bowling alley paste wax to a wood floor, then buff it with a commercial buffing machine (available at tool rental stores). The wax will restore the floor's luster and help conceal scuffs.

Choose cork floors to reduce noise.

Cork tiles, made from natural bark, dull the din in busy areas. Install a durable and handsome cork floor in a family room or children's playroom.

Consider adding wainscoting to a playroom.

Durable wood wainscoting protects walls in areas that get a lot of use, such as a children's playroom.

Mix and match stair spindles.

Instead of opting for symmetry, combine several different spindle designs on your stair railing. It's more interesting. Alternate rope turned spindles with spool patterns, for instance.

Accent your staircase.

Paint the risers on your stairs an accent color to add interest.

Vary your lighting sources.

Use different types of lighting in your living areas, both for convenience and aesthetics. A combination of ambient, task, and mood lighting is best (see Chapter 3 for more information).

Install overhead fixtures for general illumination.

Ambient light gives overall illumination for an entire space—ceiling fixtures are the most common source of ambient light.

Use task lighting for special functions.

Task lighting shines on a specific spot so you can see to perform a particular task—a reading lamp could serve this purpose. So could track lights or canisters in a kitchen.

Set the mood with mood lighting.

Mood lighting acts to accent a room or offer a soft background glow when bright lights aren't appropriate. Low-wattage lamps, wall sconces, chandeliers with candlelight bulbs, and torchieres may be used to create this effect.

FAST FIX

Here's an easy way to add variety to your lighting scheme: Place spotlights on the floor behind large floor plants and direct the beams upward, so they shine on the ceiling. The light glowing through the leaves gives the impression of sunlight through trees.

Arrange for flexible lighting.

Dimmer switches give you the best of all worlds. Use them with lamps and overhead fixtures so you can shift from ambient to task to mood lighting at the touch of a finger. Choose from lots of different dimmer designs that are less obtrusive than the old, knob-like switches.

 **SHOW & SELL**

Leave the lights on when your home is being shown to prospective buyers. It will seem more open, cheerful, and inviting.

Consider installing a wooden ceiling.

Bead board isn't just for wainscoting. Affixed onto a ceiling, it adds visual interest while concealing cracks, watermarks, or other damage.

A ceiling of acoustic tile squares may cause prospective
buyers to wonder if a leaky roof or other damage is being
concealed. Be sure to have damaged tiles replaced before
you show your home.

Decorate an acoustic tile ceiling.

If it's impractical to remove an acoustic tile ceiling, consider
transforming an eyesore into an eye-catching focal point.
Paint the tiles a single color or get creative and create a color
pattern that utilizes the grid to advantage. For example, artists
decorated the acoustic tile ceiling of the Cabot Cinema in
Beverly, Massachusetts, with a beautiful Art Deco design that's
a real show-stopper.

Consider opening up a ceiling.

A small, single-story ranch or bungalow can be made to seem

more spacious if you open up a ceiling—or part of it—into the attic area. If structural beams/joists are needed, leave them exposed and integrate them as an attractive design feature.

Consider adding a ceiling medalion.

Old mansions often featured ornate ceiling medallions in the dining room, from which a chandelier might have hung. Decorative medallions cast in synthetic materials are easy to install and instantly turn a drab ceiling into a showpiece.

FAST FIX

Hang a decorative cornice or pediment above a door or window to dress it up. Consider molded plaster, carved wood, wrought iron, or a painting done on an arched panel as an attractive accent in a spot that's usually ignored.

Hang artwork at eye level.

The center of a painting should be at your eye level—not halfway between the back of the sofa and the ceiling. If you're hanging several pictures in a grouping, the center of the arrangement should be at eye level.

FOR SALE SHOW & SELL

Before your home is shown to prospective buyers, remove artwork that some people might find objectionable—nudes, political or religious pictures, flags or military memorabilia, for instance. Some real estate agents even recommend taking down family photographs because buyers want to imagine themselves—not you—occupying the space.

Install picture rail molding.

Here's an attractive way to display your favorite works of art. Instead of simply hanging pictures on nails hammered into the walls, attach decorative molding at the top of a wall or walls. Put picture hooks into the moldings and suspend paintings from wires or cords hung on the hooks. Hint: Use fifty-pound clear fishing line for hanging artwork from a picture rail molding. It's practically invisible.

FAST FIX

Smoke alarms could save your life—install them on every floor of your home to alert you in case of fire. Battery-operated alarms are inexpensive and easy to attach to ceilings; hardwired systems usually require an electrician's expertise. Hint: Some communities require you to install smoke alarms—check with your fire department or department of public works to see what regulations apply.

Arrange your artwork before you hang it.

Before you start pounding nails into the wall, lay out your artwork on the floor. Move pictures around until you arrive at a configuration that you like. This way, you're sure to be happy with the final result.

Reflect the culture of your community.

In your remodeling and/or decorating scheme, bring in some themes from a prominent culture in your community. If you live in the Southwest, for instance, American Indian or Mexican elements could add interest to your home. Pennsylvania Dutch motifs could brighten a home in Pennsylvania; Celtic imagery might work well in Boston.

Something old, something new.

Mix and match elements from different time periods, blending old with new to create interest. A Victorian stained glass window could add color to a sleek, modern bathroom. An Art Deco floor lamp could be handsome next to a contemporary Italian sofa.

Divide and conquer.

Wide open spaces can seem impersonal and hard to "tame."
Divide a great room or family room into two or more sections
to scale them down and make them easier to decorate. Think
about possible ways you and household members might use
the space, then create a conversation area, a private reading
area, an area for games, etc.

Add columns to define your space.

Decorative columns visually divide and define sections of your
living space. They also add a touch of grandeur. Hint: Don't
skimp—choose columns that are large enough and distinctive
enough to make a statement.

Replace drapes with shutters.

Ideal for homes with country or casual décor, louvered wooden
shutters are inexpensive and easy to install. Adjustable louvers
also allow you to vary the amount of light and privacy you
desire. Shutters give an airy, uncluttered appearance in a small
room, too.

CHAPTER 8

Kitchens

Leave space beside the fridge for groceries.

Position a cabinet or work surface beside your refrigerator so you'll have a convenient place to plunk bags of groceries.

Leave open counter space on either side of the stove.
Allowing at least eighteen inches of countertop space on either side of the stove serves two purposes. You'll have room to set food, dishes, pots, etc. while you cook. You'll also provide a safety zone—leaving one side of a stove exposed increases the chance of accidental burns, especially if there are young children in the home.

Select cabinet doors of the same size.
Opt for consistency when selecting kitchen cabinets. Try to keep all the doors the same width, say fifteen or eighteen inches, on both base and upper cabinets. Align the doors up and down to create a sense of symmetry. The overall effect will be more harmonious than if you mix a variety of sizes and shapes.

Update cabinet hardware.
Replace old metal hardware with glass or porcelain knobs. This quick, inexpensive update transforms your kitchen immediately.

Avoid cabinets with glass doors.

Cabinets with glass doors are great if you have lots of pretty dishes or stemware to display, but unless you're exceptionally neat they aren't a practical choice for most kitchens. Glass doors reveal clutter and show fingerprints.

Consider adding roll-out trays to provide easy access.

If you add full-extension, roll-out trays to base cabinets, you'll never have to get down on your hands and knees and rummage around to reach something in the back. Ideal for storing pots, pans, large casserole dishes, and other heavy items, these convenient trays also let you get organized and reduce cabinet clutter.

Try snap-on shelving for under-sink storage.

Home organizing stores sell snap-on shelving systems designed specifically to fit under the kitchen sink. You don't need tools to install them and they really add useful storage space.

Tap the talents of your cabinet supplier's staff.

If you plan to purchase standard kitchen cabinets from a retail
store, building supply chain, manufacturer, or other distributor,
enlist the assistance of their staff in designing your kitchen.
Many of these providers offer trained personnel and/or computer programs that can help you draft detailed plans for your
kitchen. It's also wise to let the company's representative measure your space before you place your order, just to make
sure—that way, if there's a mistake it's their responsibility, not

yours. Sometimes there's a fee for this service, but it might be credited toward your purchase.

Choose granite countertops for elegance.

Granite countertops add a touch of luxury to a kitchen. According to experts in the field, granite countertops are one of the most popular home improvements today. Beautiful and durable, they come in a wide range of colors and patterns.

Choose quartz countertops for durable beauty.

Made from natural quartz crystal, these countertops are more durable and easier to care for than granite. They require no sealing or polishing and resist stains from red wine, coffee, tea, tomato juice, and other substances that can damage the finish on granite. Here's another idea to consider: Although manufacturers make no claims to the metaphysical properties of quartz countertops, many energy workers and healers use quartz crystals to clear, strengthen, and balance the body's vital energy field. It's possible that quartz countertops could have a positive effect on your energy, too.

Choose solid surface countertops for seamless beauty.
Solid surface countertops, such as Corian, can be fabricated so there are no visible seams at joints—an advantage over granite or quartz countertops. Although not as hard and scratch-resistant as stone, these surfaces can be sanded and repaired if they get damaged.

Choose solid surface countertops with a built-in sink.
An all-in-one solid surface countertop with built-in sink affords a sleek, seamless, harmonious look. The lipless design makes clean up easy, too.

FOR SALE SHOW & SELL

Elegant stone or solid surface countertops can be a selling point in upper-end homes. But at about $35 to $75 per square foot (plus installation), they probably won't return the investment if used in a moderately priced or starter home.

Choose tile countertops for colorful practicality.

Durable ceramic tile allows you to put hot pans and pots directly on the countertop. The color and design possibilities are almost endless, affording you the greatest versatility of any countertop material. Hint: Unless you're willing to scrub the grout with a toothbrush regularly, select a gray, brown, or dark-colored grout.

 PRODUCT PICK

SpectraLOCK grout is easy to clean and doesn't need to be sealed.

Choose plastic laminate countertops for economic practicality.

Plastic laminate (from Formica, Wilsonart, and other manufacturers) is the least expensive countertop option. This low-maintenance material comes in hundreds of colors, patterns,

and finishes to suit virtually any décor. Add a wood edge
that coordinates with your cabinets to enhance attractiveness
and durability.

FAST FIX

Laminate countertops can develop "bubbles" when the adhe-
sive that holds the plastic surface to the underlayment dries
out. To remedy this, fill a syringe with glue, carefully insert
the end under the laminate, and squeeze. Place a heavy
object on the raised area to hold it down until the glue dries.

Design a wall mural between countertops and wall cabinets.

Colorful ceramic tile combines beauty with durability when
mounted on the walls between countertops and the bottoms of
your wall cabinets. Inexpensive and easy to clean, decorative
wall tile lets you be creative. Combine plain and patterned tiles,

intersperse different shapes and colors, even design a mural. Graph your design to scale on paper before you start adhering tile to the walls.

Consider the contents of your water.

Minerals or chemicals in your water supply may adversely affect some materials. For instance, water that contains a lot of iron can leave rust stains on light-colored porcelain. In Hill Country, Texas, where I live, the lime in the water discolors stainless steel. Make sure the sinks and faucets you select are made of materials that won't be damaged by your water.

Consider replacing a double sink with a single one.
Standard double sinks usually aren't big enough to wash large pots and pans. A single, large sink that's at least fifteen inches deep may be a more practical choice.

Choose a single-lever faucet set.

A single-lever faucet lets you adjust water temperature and velocity easily with one hand. Unless you want an authentic, retro, or old-fashioned look, a single-lever kitchen faucet is usually more convenient than dual hot-and-cold handles.

Choose a tall, arched faucet set.

A faucet set with a spout that's high enough to accommodate large pots is a must if you're updating your kitchen.

 PRODUCT PICK

California Faucets makes a vintage-style faucet set called Carmel with a weathered copper finish that ages to perfection over time.

Invest in high-quality faucets.

Inexpensive faucets may not blend hot and cold water evenly. Usually higher-end faucets contain more effective mixing chambers that allow you to better control water temperature and pressure.

FOR SALE SHOW & SELL

A $600 faucet set won't add value to a starter or moderately priced home. Choose a less expensive set and use the money you save where it will have more impact.

Avoid separate spouts.

Even if you use separate hot and cold faucets for your sink, make sure they both connect to the same spout. Separate spouts for hot and cold water are inconvenient, and you might end up getting scalded.

Investigate installing a water conditioning unit.

Minerals in your water supply can damage plumbing and shorten the life span of dishwashers, water heaters, and other appliances. If you have hard water in your home, consider using a water conditioning system.

Choose colorful appliances to brighten a kitchen.

Although white, black, bisque, and stainless steel still dominate the field, appliances in cheerful colors are making a comeback. Stoves and refrigerators in yellow, red, blue, or green can add drama to your kitchen.

Paint your refrigerator.

If your refrigerator is still in good condition, but the old finish doesn't match your new kitchen's color scheme, give it a facelift. For significantly less than the cost of a new fridge you can have your old one professionally resurfaced right in your home.

 PRODUCT PICK

Big Chill makes a cool and funky, pale yellow 50s-style fridge that will remind Boomers of Mom's kitchen.

Choose a refrigerator with a freezer at the bottom.

Although refrigerators with freezers on the bottom tend to be more expensive than those with the freezer at the top, the extra cost may be justified by their extra convenience. Bottom-freezer models put the foods and drinks you use most often where they're easy to see and reach, without bending.

Change the way a refrigerator door opens.

Refrigerators doors come assembled with the handles on the left. If you want the doors to swing the other way, say so when you purchase your fridge. The store from which you purchase it can make the adjustment before the fridge is delivered. (If you're handy with tools, it's easy to change the door yourself.)

Know that two ovens are better than one.

Whether you choose a free-standing range or a built-in wall model, two ovens are better than one. People who like to cook can bake a pie in one oven and roast a turkey in the other. People who rarely cook big meals can use the smaller oven most of the time and save energy.

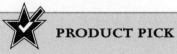
Cook with gas—and electricity.

Many cooks like the versatility and effectiveness of dual-fuel ranges. Consider upgrading your old stove to one that combines an electric oven with a gas-fired cook top.

Check out today's toaster ovens.

A toaster oven may be the perfect option for one or two people. Rather than heating up the "real" oven just to bake a brownie or a few potatoes, use the trusty toaster oven and save on your cooling bills. Today's toaster ovens are versatile enough to roast meat, bake bread, and cook casseroles.

PRODUCT PICK

With Küppersbusch's honeycomb cook top modules, you can design your own built-in cook top to suit your unique culinary needs. Each glass-ceramic hexagonal unit is approximately 1 foot in diameter and fits flush into the cooking surface. Select from a variety of dual or single-circuit zones and choose how much firepower you want each module to provide.

Save counter space with a drawer-style microwave.

Few of us can get by without the convenience of a microwave oven. But we sacrifice a big chunk of valuable counter space in exchange. Luckily, there is a solution: Instead of taking up room on your countertop, a microwave oven in a drawer can be installed under the countertop. It's convenient, yet out of the way.

PRODUCT PICK

The Whirlpool's g Microven does more than nuke your food. This single, versatile appliance lets you grill, bake, toast, roast, and simmer/steam as well.

Consider that two drawers are better than one.

Dishwashers with two separate washing compartments are ideal for small households and people on the go who don't cook or eat at home very much. Because you can fill only one section at a time with dishes and run the equivalent of half an ordinary load, two-drawer dishwashers save energy and water. Another plus: Dual washing controls let you run two loads at once and adjust the individual cleaning cycles to suit your needs. Fill one drawer with pots and pans, the other with glasses.

PRODUCT PICK

KitchenAid and Fisher & Paykel both make two-drawer dish-washers that do double duty.

Give your dishwasher a pretty face.

Many manufacturers of kitchen cabinets offer matching fronts for dishwashers. Cover up your dishwasher with panels that let it blend in with your cabinets.

FAST FIX

Remove fingerprints, watermarks, food stains, and other unsightly marks from stainless steel appliances with WD-40. Pour a little on a soft cloth and wipe stainless steel surfaces with it to clean and protect them.

Nix the garbage disposal.

If your home has a septic system instead of being hooked up to a city sewer line, a garbage disposal may not be a good idea. The bacteria that keep the septic tank operating effectively don't process uneaten food, so pouring veggie scraps and ground up eggshells into your system may overtax it. Consider composting instead. You can use the rich soil to nourish your plants.

Consider using track lighting in kitchen work areas.

Adjustable track lighting allows you to shine light where you need it most. Easy to install and inexpensive, track lighting is more attractive than florescent fixtures and more flexible than recessed canisters. Small-scale units with high-intensity halogen lights work well even in kitchens with low ceilings.

Avoid curtains in a kitchen.

Kitchens look brighter, neater, and more spacious when windows are left bare. In a busy kitchen, curtains will require frequent washing and ironing to keep them looking fresh and pretty. If privacy is an issue, replace curtains with easy-care mini-blinds. If you don't need privacy, eliminate window treatments altogether.

Hang "top-down, bottom-up" shades.

Shades and blinds that can be lowered to allow light in at the top or raised to let light in at the bottom provide maximum versatility. Install them in your kitchen to give just the right amount of light and privacy.

Choose vinyl flooring for economic practicality.

Whether you opt for squares or sheets, vinyl flooring offers practicality and affordability. With an extensive range of available colors, patterns, and textures, vinyl flooring is compatible with virtually any kitchen style. Self-adhesive vinyl squares are easy to apply; sheet vinyl requires a bit more skill.

Choose ceramic tile for beauty and durability.

Ceramic tile is easy to care for, lasts a lifetime, and enhances the appeal of any kitchen. Whether you choose Mexican-style terra-cotta for a rustic look, tiny squares for an Art Deco feel, or marble-like patterns for a sophisticated ambiance, the wide range of colors and designs offers something for everyone.

 PRODUCT PICK

Congoleum's DuraCeramic tiles made from limestone are more durable than conventional ceramic floor tiles. They're warmer and quieter to walk on, too.

Consider installing radiant heat under the kitchen floor.

Radiant heat is the ideal solution for a kitchen. It warms up cold tiles or vinyl, and because it doesn't require baseboards or air vents, you'll have more space and flexibility when it comes to configuring cabinetry.

PRODUCT PICK

EnviroGLAS floors, made of recycled glass bottles, are as durable as they are beautiful. Choose from an array of color and design options. You can even create an original one-of-a-kind floor.

Choose wood floors for casual elegance.

Early American homes usually featured wooden floors in their kitchens. Oak, fir, and hard pine are traditional woods used in old kitchens, but any hardwood could be a good choice. Seal the wood with a matte polyurethane finish to waterproof it, and a wood floor becomes a practical option as well as a beautiful one.

Don't overdo the bare wood look.

Natural wood floors look best when paired with painted cabinets. Otherwise, you can get too much of a good thing.

 PRODUCT PICK

Chemically sensitive or ecologically minded individuals will appreciate Marmoleum's sheet flooring that's made of pine resin, jute fibers, linseed oil, and other natural materials.

CHAPTER 9

Private Spaces

Bedrooms

Choose a pretty color for your bedroom ceiling.

Who says ceilings have to be white? It's more interesting to let a ceiling echo one of the colors in your furnishings—especially in the bedroom, where the ceiling is often the first thing you see when you wake up.

Use one color on your walls and ceilings.

Especially if you're using a light shade, paint the walls and ceiling the same color. This "wrap-around" technique saves time. You don't have to carefully cut in when painting the area where the walls and ceiling join.

Choose a wall to accent with color.

Choose one wall—perhaps the headboard wall or the wall you see first when you wake up in the morning—to paint in a bold accent color. You might want to experiment with decorative glazes, sponge or rag painting, stenciling, or even a mural.

Avoid switching paint cans when painting a wall.

If a room will require more than one gallon of paint, complete as many entire walls as possible from one gallon. When you near the bottom of the can, begin a new wall with a new gallon. Don't paint part of a wall from one can, then expect the paint in another can to match. Even if they were purchased at the same time, the color mix might not be exactly the same in both cans.

Save some paint for touchups.
Save a small amount of paint for touchups, but dispose of it after a year. By then the color on your walls will have faded or discolored slightly.

Design a color scheme around a favorite piece of fabric.
Start with a bedspread, curtain fabric, Oriental rug, or other patterned piece of material and base your color scheme on it. Use colors on walls, carpets, etc. in the same proportions as they are shown on your favorite piece of fabric.

Add a small fridge to your master suite.
Do you enjoy a glass of milk before bed or wake up hungry during the night? Put a small refrigerator in the master suite to keep drinks and snacks handy. Fit it into your closet or install it under your bathroom counter for convenience.

Consider moving your washer and dryer to the bed/bath suite.

Most laundry is generated in the bedrooms and baths, so it makes sense to put the washer and dryer here, rather than in a kitchen or basement.

Affix reading lights to the headboard wall.

Instead of placing lamps on the nightstands, install reading lights on the wall on either side of the bed. Hint: Fixtures with adjustable rods and dimmer switches allow versatility.

Select a few big pieces for a small room.

Filling a small room with dinky furnishings gives the impression of being in a dollhouse. Instead, select a few, attractive pieces of furniture and let them make a bold statement. Eliminate clutter, stick with solid colors instead of patterns, and reduce accessories to a minimum to keep the space from seeming cramped.

Take down the curtains in a small bedroom.

Curtains and drapes visually enclose a room. To make a small space seem larger, eliminate bulky window treatments. Instead, opt for mini-blinds, shutters, or simple fabric shades set within the window frame.

Create a sanctuary in your home.

Set aside a quiet, private spot in your home where you can retreat to enjoy peace and quiet—an attic hideaway, a nap nook built into a large bay window niche, a meditation area nestled in an alcove under eaves, or a reading corner in the master bedroom. Surround yourself with comfortable furnishings and personal treasures, things that make you feel nourished and secure. Let this private sanctuary be your own, special R&R getaway.

Consider carving out wall niches.

Wall niches—like those recessed alcoves in the walls of old missions and monasteries—are a great way to display statues, artifacts, and other treasures. They provide an interesting and attractive alternative to shelves for showcasing artwork.

Don't get stuck in symmetry.

You don't have to stick with matched bedroom sets. It's more fun to mix it up. In a child's bedroom or a guest room, use two different single beds instead of a pair, perhaps two different antique brass or iron bedsteads. Put different bedspreads on them, too. Unite the two by using the same colors.

Bathrooms

Go wild in a small bathroom.

Small baths and powder rooms can be fun places to really let your imagination soar. Select bright paint colors, faux finishes, or way-out wallpaper to make this oft-overlooked space distinctive.

Hide stains with colored bathroom fixtures.

Some water supplies contain minerals or other substances that can stain tubs, toilets, and sinks. In Central Texas, for instance, lime in the water leaves a greenish residue on porcelain and plastic. If iron is present in your water, choose red, brown, or black fixtures to prevent unsightly rust marks. Replace old white porcelain with new colors that hide stains.

FAST FIX

Use a pumice stone to remove rust or hard-water stains on porcelain toilet bowls.

Consider adding a soaking tub.

Hippocrates believed "the path to health is a scented bath and a daily massage." To indulge yourself with regular, long, soaks in a hot bath you may want to install an extra large soaking tub in your bathroom. Choose from lots of styles and options: High-backed slipper tubs, old-fashioned claw-foot tubs, free-standing pedestal tubs, extra-deep Japanese soaking tubs, and whirlpool and spa models transform an ordinary bathroom into a personal retreat.

Separate the tub and shower.

If you're designing a master suite, choose a separate tub and shower stall arrangement instead of the ordinary all-in-one combination. This attractive and versatile plan allows you to customize your bathroom to suit your individual cleansing style. Build a roomy, walk-in shower area with lots of options—body spray jets, hand-held shower, steam only, even a personal rainforest! A deep soaking tub, with or without whirlpool jets, provides soothing luxury.

Spotlight the sink.

The convention used to be to match the sink, toilet, and tub. However, it's more fun to choose a sink in a different color or material as an accent. Consider a brightly patterned porcelain sink, perhaps one painted to resemble Mexican pottery or blue-and-white Delft china. Hammered copper or pewter sinks add a handsome touch in a traditional bathroom; colored glass sinks put pizzazz in a contemporary setting.

Give an old washstand a new role.

Consider updating an antique washstand by turning it into a bathroom vanity. Hint: Choose an old-fashioned milk-white porcelain sink or one that's painted with little flowers to mimic the wash basins and pitchers that sat on washstands before the days of indoor plumbing.

FAST FIX

Give your bathroom a quick pick-me-up by changing the pulls on the vanity. Choose something colorful, whimsical, or dramatic—have fun.

Protect a marble vanity top.

Marble, with its extensive range of colors and patterns, is a lovely choice for a bathroom vanity top. But this porous material must be protected from water and other liquids to keep it looking its best. Seal it with stone or patio sealer (available in most hardware stores).

Make an antique mirror a focal point.

Instead of hanging an ordinary bathroom vanity mirror, dress up your bathroom with a unique, antique mirror above the sink, perhaps one that was designed originally to hang over a buffet or dresser. Choose one with a frame of carved wood or ornate gilt. If you're creative, you may enjoy painting the frame with flowers, geometric designs, or a faux stone finish. Or set mirrored glass into a handsome old picture frame.

Have GFCI electrical outlets installed in your bathroom.

GFCI, or ground fault circuit interrupter, electrical outlets reduce the risk of electrocution. Have them installed above the bathroom sink, outside the shower, etc. Building codes in some areas require GFCIs instead of ordinary electrical outlets to be used near any water source.

Invest in a water-saving toilet.
Flushing the toilet accounts for approximately one-quarter of all indoor water usage. Older toilets use about five to seven gallons of water per flush, compared with about one-and-a-half gallons for modern water-saving models. Many communities' building codes require that low-flow toilets be installed in new homes and when a bathroom is remodeled. Replace your antiquated, wasteful toilet with a more efficient one. The net savings could be as much as 20,000 gallons of water per toilet per year.

PRODUCT PICK

Not all water saver toilets are created equal. Those with pressure bladders are powerful and efficient, but can be noisy. High velocity flush toilets, such as Eljer's Titan with a larger-than-average flush valve, are more effective than many models on the market.

Repair a leaky toilet.

About 20 percent of all toilets leak, wasting water and money. Sometimes the solution is as simple as adjusting the float on the toilet's refill valve. Or the stopper may be getting hung up, rather than settling properly to stop water flow from the tank. Fixing a leak could save you several hundred gallons of water per day.

Install a single-lever faucet in the shower.

Instead of separate hot and cold water handles, choose a single-lever model for your shower. It's easier to operate and safer, too. Building codes in some communities require single-lever faucets be used in bathrooms to reduce the risk of scalding.

Put new handles on an old tub.

If the handles on an antique, claw-foot tub are rusted or dripping, it's easy to replace them. With a wrench, remove the old handles and stems. Before you attach the new handles, wrap the stems with plumber's tape and coat them with heat-resistant grease to help reduce wear and tear and extend their useful life.

Design a decorative tile shower stall.

Create a unique design for your shower on graph paper (make sure it's to scale), with each square representing a piece of colored tile. Mix and match solids and patterns; even render a landscape, mosaic, or other picture with tiles. When you're confident in your design, head to the home store to purchase the materials you'll need.

 PRODUCT PICK

Sandhill Industries makes beautiful glass tiles from recycled bottles. These "green" tiles require less energy to produce and save landfill space.

Purchase all the tile you'll need for the job at one time.

If you want to be sure your tile matches, purchase all the material you'll need for the job at the same time, from the same dye lot. The manufacturer may discontinue a design, or tile from a different dye lot may not match exactly. Hint: Buy some extra tiles in case you need to replace any in the future.

Choose porcelain stone tiles rather than marble.

Marble gives a bathroom an elegant appearance, but it's not as durable or stain resistant as porcelain tiles that resemble natural travertine marble. These are an attractive and practical solution for floors, walls, shower stalls, countertops, and tub surrounds.

Hide the toilet.

Position a privacy screen to hide the bathroom toilet from plain view.

Keep the lid down.

Feng shui recommends keeping the lid on the toilet seat closed, to prevent beneficial chi from going down the drain. Keeping the lid down will also keep your dog from drinking out of the toilet and your cats from jumping in!

Put a bench in your bathroom.

Provide a place in the bathroom to sit comfortably and put on your shoes, clip toenails, or perform other routine personal hygiene tasks. Benches designed for exterior use are ideal in a bathroom, because they can withstand wet conditions. An outdoor bench made of teak, cedar, wrought iron, or wicker makes an attractive and practical addition to a bath or dressing area.

FAST FIX

Hard water can leave behind mineral deposits that clog your showerhead. To clean them away, dip an old toothbrush in a mixture of baking soda and white vinegar and scrub the showerhead with the solution. Another option is to place white vinegar in a plastic bag and hang the bag so that the showerhead is immersed in the vinegar. Fasten the bag onto the showerhead with a rubber band and leave it to soak for about an hour.

Let there be light.
Consider installing a skylight above your shower to let the sun shine down on you while you wash. It's the next best thing to standing under a waterfall.

Leave some elbow room.
If you're placing the toilet next to a sink/vanity, make sure to leave enough "elbow room" between them. Eighteen inches from the edge of the sink or vanity to the center of the toilet is considered the minimum amount of space for personal comfort.

Consider wheelchair accessibility.
If your household includes elderly members or you live in a retirement community, it could be a good idea to allow extra room in a bathroom for handicapped access. Choose a toilet with a higher-than-standard seat that's easier for people with restricted movement to use, and remember to leave plenty of room for a wheelchair to move around.

Install hand rails in bathrooms.

Install hand rails in bath/shower stalls and beside the toilet, especially if seniors or physically challenged people will use your bathroom.

FAST FIX

Put up pegboards in kids' bathrooms; make it easy for them to hang up wet towels.

Choose a pedestal sink for a small powder room.

Because pedestal sinks aren't as bulky as cabinet-style vanities, they're perfect for small baths and powder rooms.

Choose a wall-mounted sink for a powder room.

Wall-hung sinks are another good choice for a small bathroom. These space-saving models fit conveniently into tight spaces—even corners. Hint: Choose a glass sink to create an illusion of spaciousness.

Hang your faucets on the wall.

Combine a wall-hung sink with wall-mounted faucets for maximum space efficiency and a sleek, sophisticated look.

FAST FIX

Remove lime deposits from around faucets quickly and inexpensively. Soak paper towels in white vinegar, then place the wet towels around the faucets and leave them there for an hour or so.

Install full-spectrum lighting in bathrooms.

Full-spectrum light bulbs give you the next-best thing to natural sunlight. Incandescent bulbs emphasize warm tones while florescent tubes tend to produce a greenish/blue glow; both types of lighting distort colors. Full-spectrum lighting renders a true color range. Many art museums and galleries use them for this reason. Replace conventional light bulbs above your bathroom vanity and sink with full-spectrum lights to give you a more accurate picture when applying makeup, hair color, etc.

Evaluate the ventilation in your bathroom.

Excessive moisture in a bathroom can damage paint and cause wallpaper to peel. Make sure your bath is well-ventilated.

 PRODUCT PICK

Panasonic's Whisper fans do their job without making a lot of noise about it.

Purchase a hand-held massage showerhead.

For ultimate versatility and a little luxury, indulge in a massage showerhead with adjustable water pressure options. A hand-held model that can be affixed to a slide bar lets you direct the spray where you want it.

Keep your towels warm.

Consider installing a drawer-style warming oven in your bathroom closet or vanity to keep towels, bathrobes, and pajamas luxuriously warm. Hint: Choose a custom drawer front to match your cabinetry.

CHAPTER 10

Workspaces

Home Office

Convert a closet into a mini-office.

A closet can quickly become a small, handy office. If the closet's interior is wide enough, place a pair of two-drawer file cabinets left and right, then lay a piece of wood, stone, glass, or plastic on top to form a double-pedestal desk.

Use lateral file cabinets instead of vertical ones.
Lateral files provide more usable storage than vertical ones. They're more convenient, too. Hanging file folders don't get lost in the back of drawers, and because the drawers aren't as deep, they don't stick out so far into the room when open. You can use the top of a lateral file cabinet as an extra work surface, too.

Consider adding built-in bookcases around a window.
Built-in bookcases provide much-needed storage in a home office and keep reference materials, computer equipment, etc. neat and convenient. Consider natural wood bookcases, as they give a home office a distinguished look, like an old English library. Configure them around a window to make the most of a wall that's already broken up.

Invest in a cozy reading nook.

Consider having a contractor build a window seat under a window to create a sunny reading nook.

Create a U-shaped work surface.

Keep everything at your fingertips. A U-shaped desk provides lots of convenient work surface that you can easily access without ever having to get up from your chair.

Control power cord clutter.

Rein in your electrical cords by housing them in plastic channels that can be mounted to your baseboards.

Label electrical cords.

Don't guess which electrical cord is which. Label them with small, individual tags that identify what connects to what.

Have ungrounded outlets replaced.

Ungrounded electrical outlets can cause power glitches that may adversely affect your computer and other equipment. Have them replaced with safer, properly grounded outlets.

Choose track lighting.

Instead of overhead fluorescents, use track lighting that lets you adjust individual lamps and focus light on specific work areas as needed.

Choose recessed ceiling lights for your home office.

Recessed canisters in your office ceiling, when positioned around the perimeter of the room, provide pleasant ambient light. Hint: Add dimmer switches so you can adjust light levels as needed.

Hang a pendant fixture over your keyboard.

Position a small halogen pendant fixture above your keyboard so it provides good task lighting without throwing unwanted glare onto your computer screen.

Don't place the computer in front of the window.

If you position the computer in front of the window, background sunlight will compete with the computer's screen. If you place the computer so that sunlight shines directly on the monitor, you'll run into problems, too. As you configure your home office, plan a spot for the computer that's away from the window.

Choose calming colors for your office.

Cool, soothing colors such as green, blue, gray, or tan are usually best for office environments, because they help reduce stress. However, if you work in a creative field, yellow or peach might be better choices because they stimulate imagination.

Hang a picture of a landscape in your office.

Relieve that boxed-in feeling. Hang a painting of a landscape with a distant view in your office. Periodically, gaze at the picture to rest your eyes, relax your mind, and visually expand your horizons. Hint: Choose photos that capture your favorite places. Photos with scenes that draw you in—a country fence-row, a Southwestern mountain setting—will open up the vista even more.

Workshop

Invest in upgrading your electricity.

Power tools use a lot of electricity. Consider upgrading your electrical system to accommodate your equipment. This also means installing numerous outlets at convenient spots in your shop so you'll have plenty of power when and where you need it.

Use rolling shelf units for practical versatility.

Steel shelving units with locking casters allow you to move them about easily when necessary. Sleek and sturdy, these versatile modules are perfect for organizing your workshop, office, garage, or pantry.

Install shelves, shelves, and more shelves.

You can't have too many shelves in a workshop, where organization is a priority. Adjustable shelves are better than stationary ones. If your garage is doing double-duty as a shop, install plenty of shelves so tools and gadgets stay neat, safe, and handy.

Hang up a workbench.
A garage or utility area can become a workshop instantly —hang a fold-down workbench on one wall. Like a Murphy bed, it closes up, out of place, when not in use.

Choose power equipment that folds up.
Some table saws, lathes, drill presses, joiners, etc. are designed to fold up and roll out of the way when not in use. If work-space is limited, a "five-in-one" that combines five different pieces of equipment into a single unit can be a convenient choice. This practical tool enables you to make the most of your shop's floor space.

Install locks on storage cabinets/closets.
Safety comes first, especially if you have young children in your home. Lock up cabinets and/or closets where you store your tools to prevent the risk of accidental injury.

Replace fluorescent lighting.

Many shops feature unimaginative overhead fluorescent lighting, but adjustable track lights offer more versatility and let you direct light where you need it most. Halogen lights provide greater clarity and less color distortion than fluorescents, too.

Hang tools on a Peg-Board.

The trusty Peg-Board is a staple in many workshops. To keep track of your tools, draw an outline of each tool on the Peg-Board, to show where it belongs. If something hasn't been put back in its proper place, you'll notice immediately.

Label your electric box.

Label the circuit breakers on your electric box to indicate which ones are linked with which functions in your home. Hint: You may also wish to draw a diagram on a separate piece of paper to show which circuit breakers operate which features in your home.

Divide your work areas.

Separate clean and dirty areas in your workshop. Build a
sawdust-free zone that can be closed off for painting,
varnishing, etc. Place house saws, lathes, joiners, and other
power equipment in another section of the workshop.

Take stock and clear the air.

Inhaling dust, paint fumes, etc. can be hazardous to your
health. Survey your workshop to make sure it has a good
ventilation system.

Consider adding a sink in your shop.

Make cleanup easy and keep dust, paint, oil, etc. out of the rest of the house with a utility sink in your workshop.

Exercise Room

Add bright colors to a workout room.

If your exercise area is dull and uninviting, you might not want to spend much time there. By adding colorful artwork or a bright coat of paint, you may be able to increase your motivation to work out. Red and orange are two great choices, as they are mentally and physically stimulating.

Add plants to the exercise area.

Healthy plants are a quick and easy way to add to the aesthetic appeal of a workout room.

Add some pleasing scents.

Burn scented candles or incense before or while you're using your workout room. Stimulating aromas such as clove and cinnamon can actually enhance your energy and focus.

Hang a full-length mirror in your workout area.

Keep an eye on your progress by hanging a full-length mirror in your exercise room. A mirror also lets you check your position to make sure you're holding that yoga posture or doing those curls correctly.

Choose lighting that emphasizes warm tones.

Fluorescent lights produce cool illumination, which is less flattering to most skin types than warm, incandescent light. To give yourself a rosy glow, use incandescent or full-spectrum light bulbs in your workout area.

Opt for versatility in your lighting plan.

Track lights or canisters recessed into the ceiling are usually the best choices for an exercise area, allowing you to direct light where you need it. This kind of lighting will also keep electrical cords from tripping you up. Plan your work out zones first, then position lighting so it illuminates each zone adequately.

Have someone install dimmer switches on your lights.

If you use your exercise area for more than one type of workout, dimmer switches will allow you to adjust lighting to suit your needs—bright lights for weight training, softer illumination for yoga or tai chi.

Choose commercial grade carpet for a workout room.

Low pile, commercial grade carpet is a good choice for a workout area. It's manufactured to stand up to heavy use, and imprints left by exercise equipment won't be as obvious as they might be on plush carpet.

PRODUCT PICK

Versatile textured foam flooring from Great Mats lets you pick up your floor and store it, conveniently, when not in use. Individual 2-by-2-foot squares interlock like pieces of a puzzle. Lay it down over concrete in a garage or basement to create a workout surface that's easy on your feet. Cleanup is a breeze, too. Just damp mop or vacuum.

Hang a hammock.

Keep your exercise gear neat and handy with a mesh gym hammock. Hang the hammock in the corner of your workout room and use it to corral clutter.

CHAPTER 11

Storage Sites

Closets

Add a clothing rod.

Here's a quick and inexpensive way to maximize your closet space: Many closets feature a single clothing rod that runs the entire width of a closet. Consider supplementing it with another full-length rod positioned higher for longer garments or lower for shirts and skirts. A lumber yard will cut a wooden rod to size for you—all you need to do is support it on brackets that fasten easily into place.

Make use of modular storage units.

Baskets, pull-out trays, shoe racks, drawers, and other modular storage elements all expand the usable space in your closet and keep clothing neat. Incorporate them into your closet plan to maximize storage potential.

Add shelves for storage.

If your closet is wide or deep, adding shelves in back or down one side can provide much-needed storage.

Consider building a cedar closet. An ordinary closet can be transformed into a cedar closet with a kit that includes interlocking pieces of aromatic cedar. If you're selling your home, this simple update makes a good impression on prospective buyers. Hint: For added moth protection, hang your wool garments on cedar hangers.

In children's closets, hang clothing rods at kid height.

Make it easy for kids to hang up their clothes by installing closet rods at a height they can reach easily. Instead of a single rod that runs the width of the closet, install two rods, one above the other, to maximize storage space. Hang off-season or rarely worn clothes on the top rod and place frequently worn garments on the lower rod.

Consider a built-in ironing board.

In older homes, ironing boards often folded into the wall when not in use. These convenient contraptions made ironing a bit less onerous and did away with the problem of where to store the ironing board. Have one built into your laundry area, a closet, pantry, or bathroom. The apparatus fits easily between the studs in a wall and everything closes up neatly, out of sight, when not in use.

Attic

Hire someone to insulate your attic.

Heat rises, so it's no surprise that an uninsulated attic is a prime source of heat loss. Not only will insulating your attic save you money in heating bills—especially as fuel costs continue to escalate in the future—experts say investments in energy-saving updates provide one of the biggest paybacks when you sell your home.

 PRODUCT PICK

Icynene foam insulation expands after being sprayed between studs to efficiently seal leaks and fill gaps. It will appeal to environmentally conscious consumers, too, because it contains no ozone-depleting chemicals.

Add shelves under the eaves.

Don't waste that valuable space under the eaves in your attic. Add shelves or a shelving system for storing things you don't use often—holiday decorations, children's school projects, off-season clothing. Shelving also lets you organize your stuff and keeps it accessible so you can find it quickly when you need it.

Take stock of your attic ventilation.

It's a fact of physics: Heat will build up in your attic unless you provide an escape route. Check your attic and make note of the ventilation. Are there windows, fans, or a ventilation system that prevents excess heat from damaging whatever you've stored there? If not, call a contractor to discuss your best options.

Don't go batty.

Or squirrely, either. Keep critters out of the attic by making sure all ventilation openings are sturdily screened and any cracks or openings (around a chimney, for example) are well sealed.

Soffit vents in the attic allow air to circulate. If these vents become blocked, heat and moisture can build up and cause problems in the roof. Make sure the vents aren't clogged with dirt or debris on the outside. Also check to see that stored items or insulation inside the attic aren't interfering with ventilation.

Consider adding dormers to your attic.

Open up your attic space. By dormering your attic, you could turn unused space into an extra bedroom, home office, kids' playroom, or a "room with a view."

Consider a pull-down staircase.

If the only way to get into your attic is through an access panel, consider installing a pull-down staircase to facilitate easy access. Unless the existing access panel is in a closet, you may be able to place the new staircase in the same location and avoid cutting an additional hole in your ceiling.

Basement

Purchase a new, energy-saving water heater.

Old water heaters may not be adequately insulated, so you waste energy keeping water hot. Replacing an outdated, inefficient water heater could save you money in the long term.

 PRODUCT PICK

Marathon makes an energy-efficient water heater with a plastic tank that won't corrode or rust. Encased in protective foam insulation with a polyurethane jacket, it keeps water hot longer and saves energy.

Insulate your hot water heater and pipes.

An inexpensive water heater blanket and some foam pipe sleeves can make a big difference in the amount of money you spend on hot water. Don't overlook this easy way to save energy.

Consider insulating your basement.

A cold, dank basement can sap heat from your home. By adding insulation under the floor, you'll keep heat in and drafts out. Spray foam insulation (such as Icynene or Bio Based Systems's soy-based insulation, not UFFI, which emits toxic gases) could be a better choice than fiberglass batting —it's easier to install and less likely to become damaged by dampness.

Invest in a dehumidifier.

Dampness is a fact of life in many basements, resulting in mold, mildew, and moisture damage to insulation and wooden joists. Consider installing a dehumidifier to reduce moisture in your basement.

Install a fan in your basement.
Sometimes all you need to keep a basement dry is good air circulation. A ceiling or wall-hung fan can help prevent moisture damage, mold, and mildew.

Hide cracks in concrete.
Use durable, all-weather concrete paint to cover up small cracks in a concrete wall, floor, or foundation.

Raise your washer and dryer.
Put a platform under your washer and dryer to make it easier to access front-loading appliances. If your basement is damp, raising your appliances will also help prevent problems caused by moisture. Some manufacturers make companion platforms for their washers and dryers, so you may want to contact them first.

Hang a fold-up laundry table.

A hinged panel can become a convenient table for folding laundry. Fasten it to a wall or fit it into a closet, where it can easily drop down when needed and fold up out of the way when you're finished.

About the Author

Skye Alexander is the author of more than twenty fiction and nonfiction books, including *10-Minute Clutter Control*, *10-Minute Clutter Control Room by Room*, *10-Minute Feng Shui*, and *10-Minute Feng Shui Room by Room*. She has also written for *Better Homes* and *Gardens*, *New Home*, *Country Home*, *HOME*, and numerous other home and garden publications. An interior designer and furniture designer since the mid-1970s, she has been renovating houses for more than twenty-five years. She lives on a cattle ranch in Hill Country, Texas with her cat, Domino.